D1249678

Fashion Knitwear for Children

Fashion Knitwear for Children

CLAIRE LACOSTE KAPSTEIN

Doubleday & Company, Inc.
GARDEN CITY, NEW YORK
1983

CANAJOHARIE LIBRARY
AND ART GALLERY

Acknowledgments

This book could not have been completed without the help of many individuals and companies. Grateful acknowledgment is made for permission to reprint the *Ice Cream Cone Baby Outfit*, "originally shown in McCall's Needlework & Crafts Magazine." Copyright © A. B. C. Needlework & Crafts Magazines, Inc.

The following yarn suppliers provided generous assistance:

Berger du Nord, Brookman and Sons, Inc., 4872 N.E. 12th Ave., Fort Lauderdale, Fla. 33334

Bucilla, 150 Meadowland Parkway, Secaucus, N.J. 07094

Chat Botte, Armen Corporation, 1281 Brevard Rd., Asheville, N.C. 28806

Coats & Clark, P.O. Box 48266, Atlanta, Ga. 30362

Pingouin Corporation, P.O. Box 100, Jamestown, S.C. 29453

Plymouth Yarn Co., 500 Lafayette St., Bristol, Pa. 19007

Reynolds Yarn, General Offices, 15 Oser Ave., Hauppauge, N.Y. 11788

I also wish to thank Ethan, Anne, and Laura Kapstein, Dorothy Kapstein, and my editor, Louise Gault. Larry Maglott took the great photographs. Anne and her friend Adrian Ruyle were the models.

Claire Lacoste Kapstein

Photographs by Larry Maglott
Diagrams by Claire Lacoste Kapstein
Design by Beverley Vawter Gallegos

Library of Congress Cataloging in Publication Data
Kapstein, Claire Lacoste.
Fashion knitwear for children.
Includes index.
1. Knitting—Patterns.   2. Children's Clothing.
I. Title.
TT825.K355   1983   746.9'2   82-45329
ISBN: 0-385-18204-X
Copyright © 1983 by Claire Lacoste Kapstein
Printed in the United States of America
All rights reserved
First edition

746.9
KAP

TO MY PARENTS

CAMILLE AND JACQUES

Contents

Introduction

Children are precious. In these days of the "blue-jeans uniform," we tend to forget how lovely they look in beautiful clothes. Yet children, like adults, love to dress up for parties and holidays. By donning special clothes, they gain taste and self-respect. And they're so happy when complimented on an outfit!

I am from Europe, where children's fashions are important. Many people make "fashion knitwear" for their little ones, and you see them knitting on buses, in cafés, and, of course, at home. Homemade clothes are regarded not just as a precious heirloom, but as part of the everyday wardrobe.

The clothes in this book reflect my belief that fashion should be comfortable, attractive, and easy to care for. Further, all the rich looks presented here are surprisingly affordable. Of course, the price of each garment will vary according to the yarn you purchase.

Another unique aspect of these designs is their flexibility. When an age range is given for a garment, this often indicates not only the sizes it will fit but also the fact that the outfit "grows" with the child. Thus, a long robe becomes a short dress, a dress becomes a tunic. The comments preceding each design show how the clothes are worn. Your child will enjoy these outfits not just for a few months, but for several years. Of course, knitwear is so durable that hand-me-downs are guaranteed!

Today, the variety of colors and textures available from yarn manufacturers makes knitting an exciting art. There are also an unlimited number of pattern stitches from which to choose. The designs presented here are a starting point for your imagination. Substitute yarns, colors, or stitches as you wish.

Most of the designs in the book can be made by knitters of even limited experience. The most basic pattern stitches are used, including stockinette, garter, and ribbing. The jacquard motifs are easily executed. Stunning clothes needn't be complicated to make. The impact here is on color, texture, styling, and the overall "look" of a garment.

Before you pick up your needles, I suggest that you first consult the "How-To Section" in the back. Here I have included many hints that will speed a project along. *Also, always knit a gauge before embarking on a design.* This will save hours of frustration.

I know that parents and grandparents are hard-pressed to find the time to make clothes—I'm in the same boat! But I do find it worthwhile to devote some of my evening hours and weekends to making clothes for my family. The "New Clothes from Old" can be made in just a few hours. There are many lovely, inexpensive, and quick projects included here.

Homemade clothes give pleasure both to the maker and the child. And, one day, you'll be proud to share your handicraft skills with the kids, boys and girls alike. (Remember: men have long knitted. Think of sailors!) But the greatest feeling comes when you see your little ones all dressed up and ready to go.

Good Knitting!

Baby Clothes and Accessories

A Simple Layette

Here's a perfect baby gift. It's easy to make and practical for the baby's parents: They can toss it in the washing machine when dirty. The baby will be comfortable year-round in the garment, and will look great too!

Size: 6 to 9 months.

Materials: Acrylic medium-weight yarn, 3.5 oz each white (W) and red (R). Knitting needles Nos 3, 4, and 5. Stitch holders. One Velcro (R) button. Sixteen inches of ½-inch-wide elastic for pants. Three buttons for booties and bonnet.

Pattern stitch: Pat 1: garter st: K every row. Pat 2: St st: K 1 row, P 1 row. Pat 3: checkerboard pattern: *Rows 1 and 3:* *K 3R, K 3W, rep from * across row. *Rows 2 and 4:* *P 3R, P 3W, rep from * across row. *Rows 5 and 7:* *K 3W, K 3R, rep from * across row. *Rows 6 and 8:* *P 3W, P 3R, rep from * across row.

Gauge: 22 sts = 4 inches = 40 rows (No 5 needles and Pat 1).

Finished measurements: Sweater: chest, 20 inches. Pants: waist, 16 inches.

Note: Sweater is knitted in one piece.

SWEATER

Starting at lower front edge, with No 4 needles and R, cast on 51 sts. In Pat 1 work for 12 rows. Change to No 5 needles and Pat 3 and work for 6½ inches.

SLEEVES: Change to W and Pat 1. Cast on 30 sts on each side, work even for 18 rows. Rep a second sleeve the same way. **Neck opening:** Change to R, place first 48 sts on holder, bind off 15 center sts and work on last 48 sts (half side). Continue each side separately. **Neck-opening shaping:** Bind off 3 sts at beg of next 2 rows. Dec 1 st at neck edge, every other row, 3 times. In Pat 1 work even for 14 rows. Change to W and work for 8 rows.

HALF BACK: Cast on 20 sts on neck opening side (= 60 sts). Work Pat 1 for 32 rows. *Next row:* Bind off 30 sts of sleeve. Continue work on rem 30 sts and work even until piece measures 5½ inches from sleeve. *Next row:* Change to No 4 needles and R, work for 12 rows. Bind off sts loosely.

SECOND HALF BACK: Work same as for first half back, reversing shaping. **Neckband:** With No 4 needles and R, pick up 86 sts around neck opening. In Pat 1 work for 4 rows. Change to No 3 needles and work for 6 rows. Bind off sts tightly. **Sleeveband:** With No 3 needles and R, pick up 38 sts along sleeve lower edge. In Pat 1 work for 8 rows. Bind off sts.

FINISHING: Sew side and underarm seams. Sew Velcro (R) button on each upper edge of half back. Steam lightly.

PANTS

BACK: First leg: With No 4 needles and W, cast on 24 sts. In Pat 1 work for 8 rows. Change to R and work for 2½ inches. Place sts on holder. Second leg: Work same as for first leg. **Crotch:** K across 24 sts of first leg, cast on 6 sts, and K across 24 sts of second leg (= 54 sts). In Pat 1 work even for 4 inches. *Next row:* Dec 1 st on each side of the two center sts, every 6 rows, 3 times (= 48 sts). Continue work even until piece measures 8 inches in total length. Place sts on holder.

FRONT: Work same as for back. **Waistband:** With No 4 needles and R, place back and front tog on same needle. Work in St st in reverse (purl side on right side of work) for 1½ inches. Bind off sts loosely.

FINISHING: Sew side and underleg seams. Sew a ¾-inch hem around waist. Run elastic through, adjusting to desired fit.

BONNET

Starting at front edge, with No 4 needles and R, cast on 78 sts. In Pat 1 work for 4½ inches. *Next row:* Bind off 28 sts on each side. Continue work on 22 center sts. *Next row:* K 2 tog, K 20, K 2 tog (= 20 sts). Work even until piece measures 9 inches in total length. *Next row:* K 2 tog across row (= 10 sts), K 2 more rows. Bind off sts.

FINISHING: Sew seam on each side. **Neckband:** With No 3 needles and W, cast on 12 sts, pick up 60 sts along lower bonnet edge, cast on 12 sts at end of row (= 84 sts). In Pat 1 work for 4 rows. *Next row:* On left edge border: K 4 sts, work buttonhole of 2 sts, K across. *Next row:* Cast on 2 sts over bound-off sts. Work 4 more rows. Bind off sts loosely. Sew one button on right-edge border facing buttonhole.

BOOTIES

With No 4 needles and R, cast on 32 sts. In Pat 1 work for 6 rows. Change to W and Pat 2. Work for 2½ inches. **Instep shaping:** Place first 11 sts on holder, join W and K 10 center sts, place 11 rem sts on second holder. In Pat 2 continue work on 10 center sts for 18 rows. **Foot shaping:** Right side: With R, K 11 sts from first holder, pick up 9 sts on side of instep, K 10 sts of instep of foot, pick up 9 sts on second side of instep and K last 11 sts from second holder (= 50 sts). In Pat 1 work for 12 rows (= 6 ridges). **Sole shaping:** *Dec 1 st on each side of two center sts, and 1 st at beg and at end of row, rep from * 2 more times. Bind off rem 38 sts. **Strap:** With No 3 needles and R, cast on 48 sts. In Pat 1 work 2 rows. At end of third row, work a buttonhole of 2 sts at 3 sts from end of row. *Next row:* Cast on 2 sts over bound-off sts. Work 3 more rows. Bind off sts loosely.

FINISHING: Sew sole and back seams. Sew strap on back seam. Sew button to outer edge facing buttonhole.

Easy Sleepwear

This elegant sea-blue jumpsuit is knitted in a simple ribbed pattern with soft baby yarn. Special buttons, such as the shells used here, give an added touch. The look is fresh yet classic.

Size: 3 to 6 months.

Materials: Acrylic lightweight baby yarn, 5.25 oz sea-blue. Knitting needles No 4. Stitch holders. Five shells or decorative buttons ¼-inch in diameter.

Pattern stitch: Pat 1: rib 1/1: *K 1, P 1, rep from * across row. Pat 2: brioche rib: *Row 1:* K. *Row 2:* (right side of work) *K 1, K into stitch below, rep from * across row. Rep. rows 1 and 2.

Gauge: 22 sts = 4 inches = 27 rows (No 4 needles and Pat 2).

Finished measurements: Total length, 18 inches; chest, 21½ inches.

Starting at lower edge of one leg, with No 4 needles cast on 50 sts. Work Pat 1 for 1 inch (= 12 rows). *Next row:* Change to Pat 2, inc 10 sts evenly spaced across row (= 60 sts). Work even for 8 inches. **Crotch shaping:**   Dec 1 st on one side, every other row, twice (= 58 sts). Work even in Pat 2 until 14½ inches in total length. Place sts on holder. Work a second leg the same way, reversing crotch shaping. Join two legs tog on same needle (= 116 sts). **Divide work as follows:**   Place first 29 sts on holder, keep 58 center sts on needle, and place last 29 sts on second holder.

BACK: Continue work on 58 sts. In Pat 2 work until piece measures 18 inches in total length. *Next row:* Bind off sts loosely.

HALF FRONT: Work on first 29 sts from holder. In Pat 2 work until piece measures 16½ inches in total length. Neck-opening shaping: At neck edge: Bind off 4 sts. Bind off 2 sts. Dec 1 st. Continue work even until piece measures 18 inches in total length. *Next row:* Bind off rem sts loosely. Work **second Half Front** the same way, reversing neck-opening shaping.

SLEEVES: Cast on 38 sts. In Pat 1 work for 1 inch. Change to Pat 2. *Next row:* Inc 8 sts evenly spaced across row. In Pat 2 work even for 2 inches. *Next row:* Inc 1 st on each side (= 48 sts). Continue work even until sleeve measures 6 inches in total length. *Next row:* Bind off sts loosely. Rep a second sleeve the same way.

FINISHING: Leaving upper body sides open, sew side and underleg seams. Sew lower back seam with invisible seam. Sew sleeve seams. Set in sleeves. **Right front border:** Pick up 58 sts along front edge. In Pat 1 work for 8 rows. Bind off sts in ribbing. **Left front border:** Pick up 58 sts along front edge. In Pat 1 work for 3 rows. *Next row:* Work 5 buttonholes of 2 sts (see How-To Section) spaced every 10 sts. *Next row:* Cast on 2 sts over bound-off sts. In Pat 1 work even for 3 more rows. Bind off sts in ribbing. Sew shells or buttons on right-front border facing buttonholes. **Neckband:** Pick up 64 sts along neck edge. In Pat 1 work even for 8 rows. Bind off sts loosely in ribbing. Fold neckband outside. Sew with invisible seam.

Jet-Setter Baby

Get your baby and go! The all-year-travel bunting and aviator hats are practical and fun. Nowadays people are going more places and doing more things with baby. There's no reason why he or she shouldn't go in style!

Size: 3 to 6 months.

Materials: Acrylic sport-weight yarn, 2-oz ball, 2 oz each pink (A), blue (B), light blue (C), light pink (D), yellow (F), and mint (E). Knitting needles Nos 5 and 6; 16-inch circular needle No 4. Twelve inches of 1-inch-wide Velcro (R) strip.

Pattern stitch: Pat 1: seed st: *Row 1:* *K 1, P 1, rep from *. *Row 2:* *P 1, K 1, rep from *. Rep rows 1 and 2.

Gauge: 22 sts = 4 inches = 32 rows (No 6 needles and Pat 1).

Finished measurements: Total length, 21 inches; chest, 26 inches.

BUNTING

BACK: With No 5 needles and A, cast on 74 sts. Work Pat 1 for 2½ inches. *Next row:* Change to B, dec 1 st on each side. Work even until 6 inches in total length. *Next row:* Change to C, work for 2 inches. *Next row:* Change to D, dec 1 st on each side. Work even for 2 inches. *Next row:* Change to E, work until 14 inches in total length. **Raglan shaping:**   *Next row:* Change to F. Bind off 3 first sts at beg of next 2 rows. Bind off 2 sts at beg of next 2 rows. Dec 1 st on each side, every other row, 17 times. *Next row:* Bind off rem 24 sts.

FRONT: Work same as for back until piece measures 6 inches in total length. **Opening shaping:**   Place 33 sts of right side on holder. Continue on 39 sts of left side. Work color pat as for back until piece measures 14 inches in total length. **Raglan shaping:**   Work same as for back until piece measures 18 inches in total length. **Neck-opening shaping:**   On right side of work: Bind off 5 sts, every other row, 3 times. Work on rem 33 sts. On left edge: Cast on 6 sts (= 39 sts). Work same as for other side, reversing raglan shaping and neck-opening shaping.

SLEEVES: With No 5 needles and C, cast on 32 sts. In Pat 1 work for 1 inch. *Next row:* Change to D. In Pat 1 work for 4 rows. *Next row:* Inc 1 st on each side (= 34 sts). Work even for 2½ inches. *Next row:* Change to E. In Pat 1 work for 4 rows. *Next row:* Inc 1 st on each side (= 36 sts). Work even for 3½

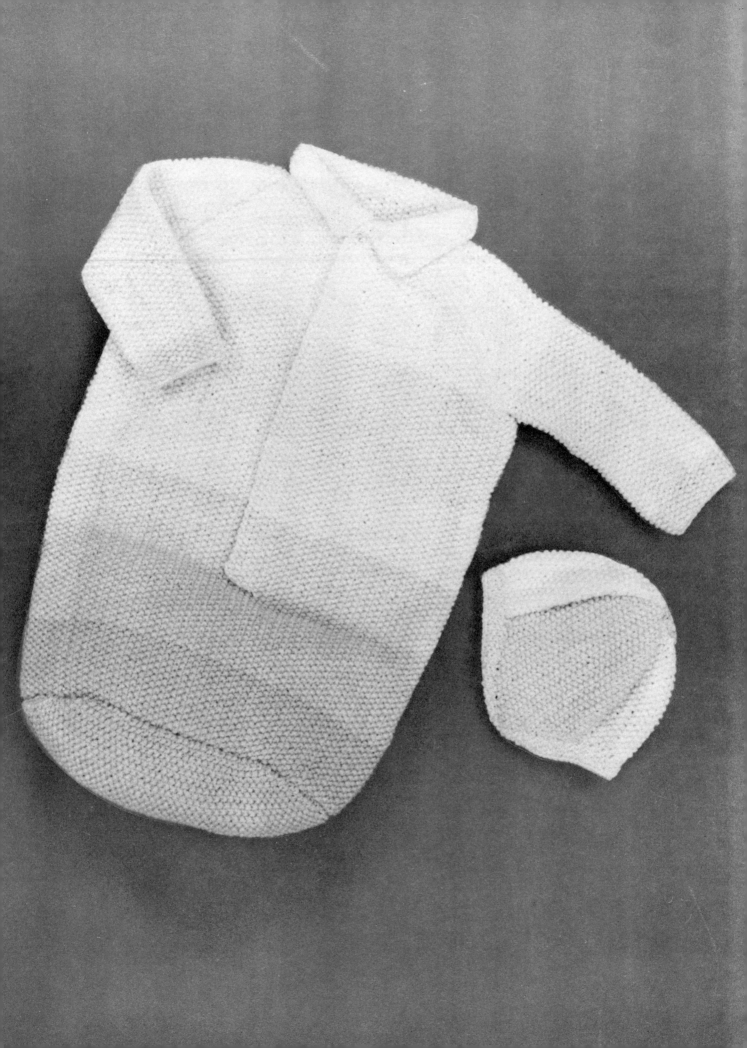

inches. **Raglan shaping:** Change to F, dec 1 st at beg of next 2 rows, 6 times. Dec 1 st at beg of next 4 rows 4 times. Bind off 2 sts at beg of next 2 rows twice. Bind off 4 sts at beg of next 2 rows. Rep a second sleeve the same way.

BOTTOM PIECE: With No 6 needles and A, cast on 24 sts. Work Pat 1. *Next row:* Inc 1 st on each side, every other row, 5 times. *Next row:* Inc 2 sts on each side, every other row, twice (= 42 sts). Work even in Pat 1 until piece measures 8½ inches in total length. *Next row:* Bind off 2 sts, on each side, every other row twice. *Next row:* Dec 1 st on each side, every other row, 5 times. *Next row:* Bind off rem 24 sts.

FINISHING: Sew side and sleeve seams. Sew Raglan seams. Sew bottom piece to body with flat seam. Sew Velcro (R) strip on inside edge of each front.

COLLAR: With No 5 needles and F, pick up 64 sts evenly along neck edge (20 sts on each front side and 24 sts on back). Work Pat 1 for 14 rows. *Next row:* Bind off sts loosely.

HAT

BACK PIECE: With No 5 needles and D, cast on 14 sts. Work Pat 1 for 2 rows. *Next row:* Inc 1 st on each side (= 16 sts). Work even in Pat 1 for 2¾ inches. *Next row:* Dec 1 st on each side, every other row, until 2 sts are left. *Next row:* Bind off.

FRONT PIECE: With No 5 needles and F, cast on 24 sts. Work in Pat 1 until piece measures 2¾ inches. *Next row:* Dec 1 st on each side, every other row, until 2 sts are left. *Next row:* Bind off.

SIDE PIECE: With No 5 needles and C, cast on 2 sts. *Next row:* Inc 1 st on each side, every other row, 11 times (= 24 sts). Work even in Pat 1 until piece measures 4½ inches. *Next row:* Dec 1 st on each side, every other row, 11 times. *Next row:* Bind off rem 2 sts. In B, work a second piece the same way.

FINISHING: Sew 4 pieces tog with invisible seam. **Hat border:** With circular needle and E, pick up 100 sts evenly along lower edge. Work 5 rounds. Next round: Bind off sts loosely.

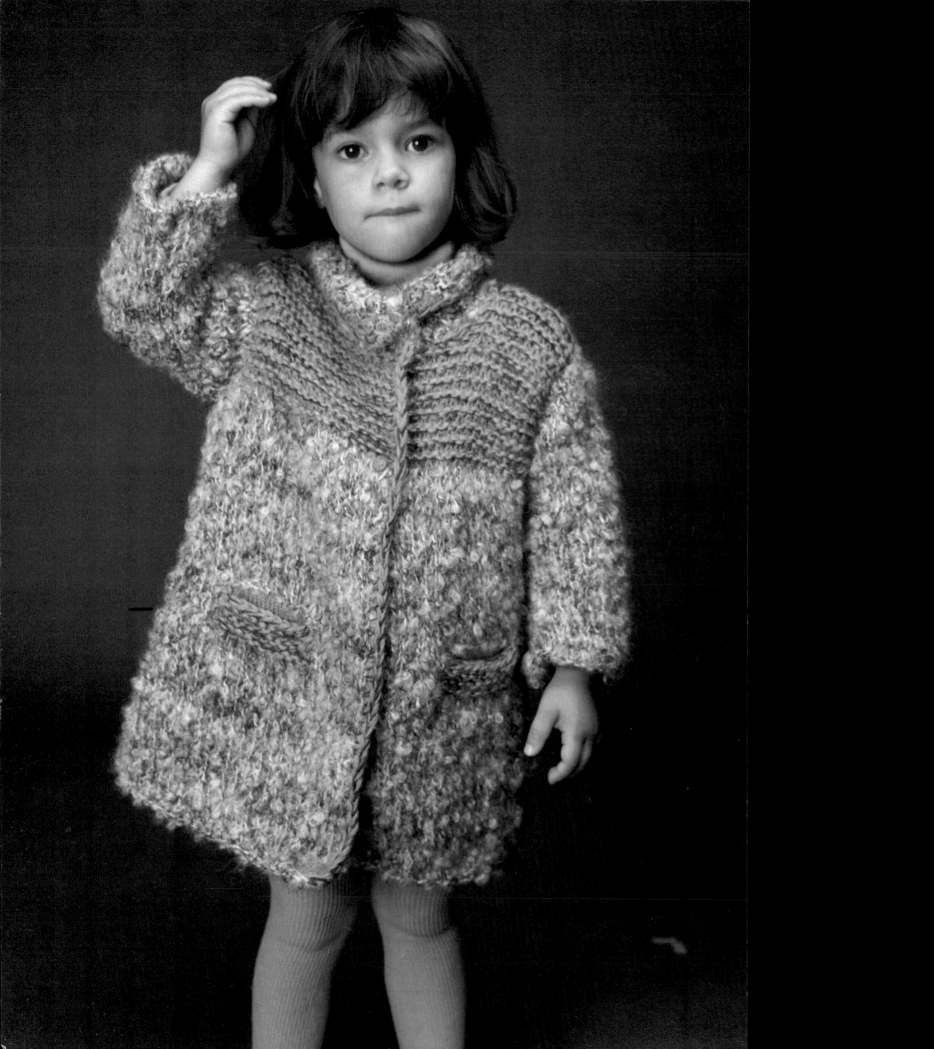

Ice Cream Cone Baby

This inviting set includes sweater, pants, booties, hat, coverlet, and a tasty toy rattle.

Size: 6 months.

Materials: Acrylic sport-weight yarn, 10 oz white (A) and 2 oz each mint (B), pale yellow (C), pale pink (D), and blue (E). Knitting needles Nos 5 and 6. Stitch holders. One Velcro (R) button for sweater. Elastic thread for pants.

Pattern stitch: Pat 1: garter st and color pat: Work 2 rows each of B, C, D, and E. Pat 2: St st: *K 1 row, P 1 row, rep from *.

Gauge: 21 sts = 4 inches = 40 rows (No 5 needles and Pat 1). 20 sts = 4 inches = 27 rows (No 6 needles and Pat 2).

Finished measurements: Sweater: total length, 8½ inches; chest, 20 inches. Pants: total length, 8½ inches; waist, 18 inches.

SWEATER

Starting at lower edge, with No 5 needles and B, cast on 114 sts. In Pat 1 work color pat. Change to No 6 needles and A. In Pat 2 work for 8 rows. *Next row:* Start jacquard motif: K across first 57 sts, join C and K 1, work across last 57 sts. Continue to follow chart until piece measures 7½ inches in total length. *Next row:* Divide work as follows: With A, K first 32 sts (half back), join a new ball of A, bind off next 4 sts (underarm). Continue on rem 42 center sts, join second ball of A, bind off next 4 sts (underarm). Continue on rem 32 sts (second half back). Work each side separately. **Armhole shaping:** At each armhole edge dec 1 st, every other row, 3 times. *Next row:* Place first 29 sts (first half back) and last 29 sts (second half back) on separate holders.

SLEEVES: With No 5 needles and B, cast on 30 sts. In Pat 1 work color pat. Change to No 6 needles and A. Inc 1 st on each side every 10 rows, 4 times (= 38 sts). Work even until sleeve measures 7½ inches in total length. **Cap shaping:** Bind off 2 sts at beg of next 2 rows. Dec 1 st at beg of next 2 rows, every other row, 3 times. Place rem 28 sts on holder. Rep a second sleeve the same way.

YOKE: Place first 29 sts (left half back), 28 sts of first sleeve, 36 sts (front), 28 sts of second sleeve, and last 29 sts (right half back) on same No 5 needle (= 150 sts). *Next row:* On right side of work: With A, K 2 tog across row (= 75

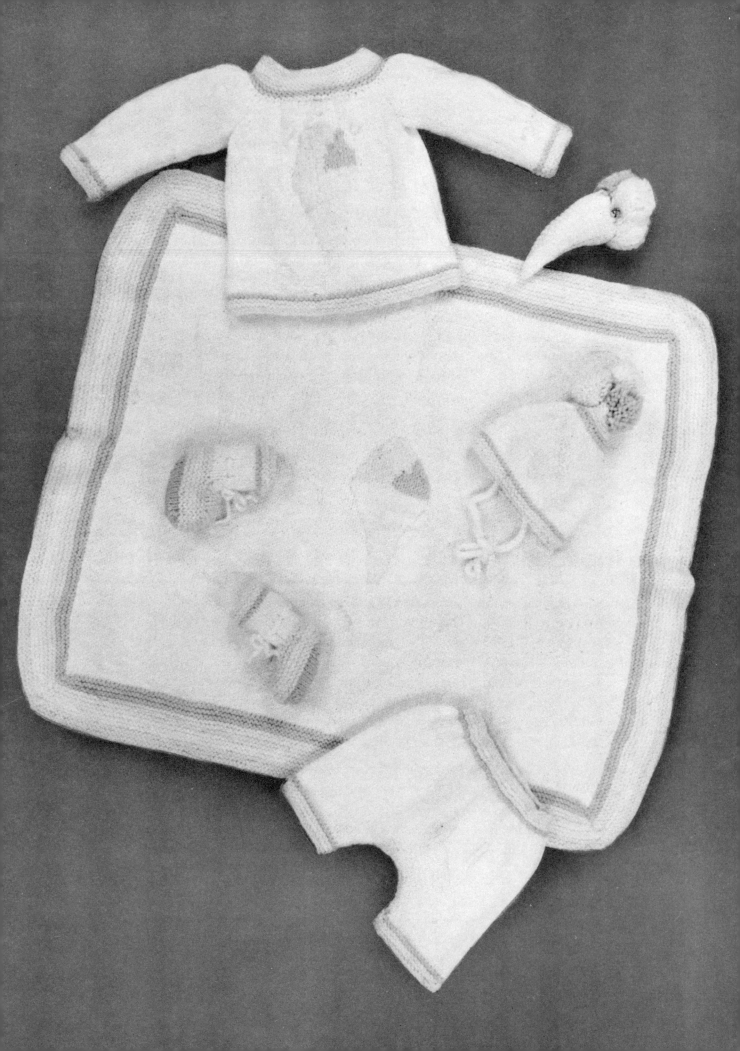

sts). *Next row:* K across. *Next row:* Work color pat working 4 rows each E, D, C, and B. Bind off all sts.

FINISHING: Sew sleeve and underarm seams. Sew Velcro (R) button on each upper edge of half back.

PANTS

LEGS: Starting at back lower edge of one leg, with No 5 needles and B, cast on 21 sts. In Pat 1 work color pat. Change to No 6 needles and A. Work for 4 rows. **Crotch shaping:** On inside edge, inc 1 st, every other row, 3 times. Cast on 5 sts. Place 29 sts on holder. **Second leg:** Work same as for first leg, reversing shaping incs.

BACK: With No 6 needles and A, K across 29 sts of first leg and 29 sts of second leg (= 58 sts). Continue work in Pat 2 for 6 inches. **Waistband:** *Next row:* K 2 tog, *K 5, K 2 tog, rep from * 8 times (= 49 sts). *Next row:* P across. Change to No 5 needles. In Pat 1 work color pat, working 2 rows each E, D, C, and B. Bind off sts.

FRONT: Work same as for back.

FINISHING: Sew side and underleg seams. On wrong side of waistband, weave elastic thread, gathering waist to desired fit.

HAT

With No 5 needles and B, cast on 60 sts. In Pat 1 work color pat. Change to No 6 needles and A. In Pat 2 work for 3 inches. *Next row:* On right side of work: *K 2 tog, K 8, rep from * 6 times (= 54 sts). Work even for 3 rows. *Next row:* *K 2 tog, K 8, rep from * 5 times, end K 4 (= 49 sts). *Next row:* P across row. *Next row:* *K 2 tog, K 6, rep from * 6 times, end K 1 (= 43 sts). *Next row:* P across now. *Next row:* *K 2 tog, K 6, rep from * 5 times, end K 3 (= 38 sts). *Next row:* P across row. *Next row:* *K 2 tog, K 5, rep from * 5 times, end K 3 (= 33 sts). *Next row:* P across row. *Next row:* *K 2 tog, K 5, rep from * 4 times, end K 5 (= 29 sts). *Next row:* P across row. Continue work even until piece measures 4³/₄ inches in total length. Work color pat as follows: *Next row:* Change to No 5 needles and E, K 2 rows. *Next row:* *K 2 tog, K 3, rep from * 5 times, end K 4 (= 24 sts). *Next row:* K across row. *Next row:* Change to D. K 2 rows. *Next row:* *K 2 tog, K 3, rep from * 4 times, end K 4 (= 20 sts). *Next row:* K across row. *Next row:* Change to C. K 2 rows. *Next row:* K 2 tog 5 times (= 15 sts). *Next row:* K across row. *Next row:* Change to B. K 2 rows. *Next row:* *K 2 tog, K 2, rep from * 3 times, end K 3 (= 12 sts). *Next row:* K across row. *Next row:* K 2 tog across (= 6 sts). Cut yarn, draw yarn through rem 6 sts. Fasten off.

FINISHING: Sew center seam with invisible seam. **Pompons:**   Work 3 pompons 2 inches in diameter in following B, D, and E. Sew pompons on top of hat. **Ties:**   With crochet hook and A, work 2 chs each 13 inches long. Sew tie on each side of hat.

BOOTIES

With No 5 needles and B, cast on 25 sts. In Pat 1 work color pat. Change to No 6 needles and A. In Pat 2 work for 1¼ inches. *Eyelet row:* On right side of work: *K 2 tog, yo, rep from * across row, end K 1 (= 25 sts). *Next row:* P across row. Continue work in Pat 2 until 2¼ inches from color pat.

INSTEP SHAPING: Place first 9 sts on holder, join B, and K 7 center sts, place last 9 sts on second holder. In Pat 1 continue work on 7 center sts for 14 rows.

FOOT SHAPING: Right side: With B, K 9 sts from first holder, pick up 8 sts on side of instep, K 7 sts of instep, pick up 8 sts on second side of instep, K 9 sts from second holder (= 41 sts). In Pat 1 work color pat working 4 rows each B, C, and D.

SOLE SHAPING: Change to E and Pat 2. *Next row:* Right side: K 3, K 2 tog, K 11, K 2 tog, K 5, K 2 tog, K 11, K 2 tog, K 3 (= 37 sts). *Next row:* P across row. *Next row:* K 3, K 2 tog, K 9, K 2 tog, K 5, K 2 tog, K 9, K 2 tog, K 3 (= 33 sts). *Next row:* P across row. *Next row:* K 2, K 2 tog, K 9, K 2 tog, K 3, K 2 tog, K 9, K 2 tog, K 2 (= 29 sts). *Next row:* P across row. *Next row:* P across row. Bind off rem 29 sts.

FINISHING: Sew sole and back seam. **Ties:**   With crochet hook and A, ch 80. Fasten off. Weave tie to each eyelet row.

COVERLET

With No 5 needles and B, cast on 130 sts. In Pat 1 work color pat working 6 rows each B, C, D, and E. Dec 1 st on each side, every 4 rows, 3 times (= 124 sts). Change to No 6 needles and A. Work even in Pat 2 until piece measures 24 inches in total length. Change to No 5 needles. In Pat 1 work color pat working 6 rows each E, D, C, and B. Inc 1 st on each side, every 4 rows, 3 times (= 130 sts). Bind off all sts loosely.

EDGING: With No 5 needles and E, pick up 124 sts along one edge in A. In Pat 1 work color pat working 6 rows each E, D, C, and B. Inc 1 st on each side, every 4 rows, 3 times (= 130 sts). Bind off all sts loosely. Rep second edging the same way on fourth edge of coverlet.

FINISHING: Join and weave corners. Ice cream cone motif: Following chart, work a separate motif. Sew to center of coverlet with invisible seam.

RATTLE

With No 5 needles and C, cast on 4 sts. In Pat 1 work for 4 rows. Inc 1 st on each side, every other row, 3 times. Inc 1 st on each side, every 4 rows, 8 times (= 26 sts). Continue work even until piece measures 4 inches in total length. Bind off 3 sts at beg of next 6 rows. Bind off rem 8 sts.

FINISHING: Fold cone in half. Sew with invisible seam. Stuff cone. Work 3 pompons 2 inches in diameter in following B, D, and E. Sew pompons on top of cone.

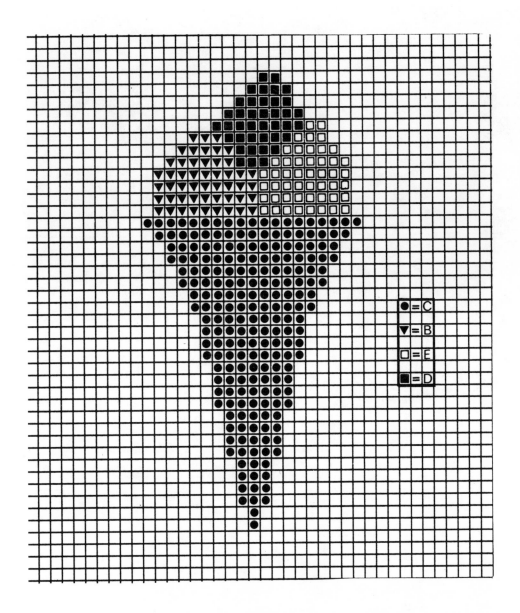

● = C
▼ = B
□ = E
■ = D

Baby Candy Suit

Delicious! That's the only word for this luxurious wool/mohair outfit flavored in caramel, raspberry, and mint. The backflap is practical, and the set includes a bonbon bonnet.

Size: 9 to 18 months.

Materials: Wool/mohair medium-weight yarn, 5.25 oz natural (MC), 1.75 oz each raspberry (B), mint (C), caramel (D). Knitting needles No 4. Stitch holders. Five small color-assorted buttons, 8 inches of 1-inch-wide Velcro (R) strip.

Pattern stitch: Pat 1: garter st: K every row. Pat 2: St st: K 1 row, P 1 row.

Gauge: 30 rows = 4 inches = 22 sts (No 4 needles and Pat 2).

Finished measurements: Total length, 24 inches; chest, 22 inches.

Note: Body is knitted in one piece, with added sleeves and a separate bonnet.

Starting at lower edge of one leg, with No 4 needles and B, cast on 64 sts. In Pat 1 work 6 rows. *Next row:* Change to C. Work 6 rows. *Next row:* Change to D. Work 6 rows. *Next row:* Change to MC and Pat 2. *Next row:* Dec 4 sts evenly spaced across row. Work even for 8 inches. Place sts on holder. Work second leg the same way. *Next row:* Join two legs tog on same needle (= 120 sts). In MC and Pat 2 work even for 2 inches. *Next row:* Place first and last 35 sts on holders. On 50 middle sts (backflap), work even for 1½ inches. *Next row:* Change to B and Pat 1. Work for 12 rows. *Next row:* Change to C and work for 12 rows. *Next row:* Change to D. K first 2 and last 2 sts of row tog. Work even for 10 rows. *On next row:* K first 2 and last 2 sts tog. Work 1 more row. Bind off rem 46 sts. Take 35 sts from first holder and cast on 50 sts in middle; take last 35 sts from second holder (120 sts on needle). In MC and Pat 2 work even for 1¾ inches. Front-opening shaping: *On right side of work*, bind off 4 sts (buttonholes side). *On left side of work*, inc 4 sts. In MC and Pat 2, work even on all sts for 6½ inches.

BACK: Place 29 first sts on holder. K 58 center sts (back), place 33 rem sts on second holder. In MC and Pat 2, work even for 4½ inches. *Next row:* Bind off sts loosely.

RIGHT FRONT: In MC and Pat 2, work even on first 29 sts for 3½ inches. Neck-opening shaping: *On neck edge*, bind off 3 sts, every other row, twice; 2 sts, every other row, once; dec 1 st, every other row, twice. Work 2 more rows. *Next row:* Bind off rem 19 sts.

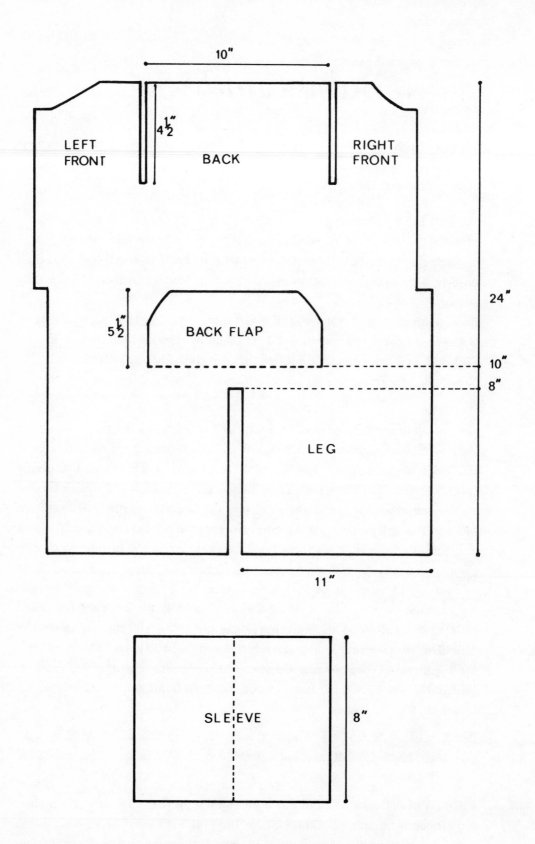

LEFT FRONT: With MC and Pat 2, work even on rem 33 sts for 3½ inches. **Neck-opening shaping:** *On neck edge,* bind off 5 sts, every other row, once; 4 sts, every other row, once; 3 sts, every other row, once; dec 1 st, every other row, twice. Work 2 more rows. *Next row:* Bind off rem 19 sts.

RIGHT-FRONT BORDER: In D pick up 50 sts along right front edge. Work Pat 1 for 3 rows. *Next row:* Work 5 buttonholes of 2 sts each (making first and last buttonholes after first 4 sts and before last 4 sts). *Next row:* Change to C. Work Pat 1 for 4 rows. *Next row:* Change to B. Work Pat 1 for 3 rows. *Next row:* Bind off sts loosely.

SLEEVES: In B cast on 46 sts. Work Pat 1 for 28 rows. *Next row:* Change to C. Work Pat 1 for 26 rows. *Next row:* Change to D. Work Pat 1 for 26 rows. *Next row:* Bind off sts loosely. Rep a second sleeve the same way.

FINISHING: Sew sides, leaving upper body open for sleeve. Sew underleg seams. Sew shoulders and sleeve seams. Set in sleeves. **Neck edge border:** With D pick up 66 sts around neck-opening edge. Work Pat 1 for 2 rows. *Next row:* Change to C. Work Pat 1 for 2 rows. *Next row:* Change to B. Work Pat 1 for 1 row. *Next row:* Bind off sts loosely. Sew buttons on left border opposite to buttonholes. Sew Velcro (R) strip on inner edge of backflap and over back side.

BONNET

FRONT: With No 4 needles and B, cast on 80 sts. Work Pat 1 for 6 rows. *Next row:* Change to C. Work Pat 1 for 6 rows. *Next row:* Change to D. Work Pat 1 for 6 rows. *Next row:* Change to MC. Work Pat 2 for 5 inches. *Next row:* Bind off sts.

BACK PIECE: With B, cast on 19 sts. Work Pat 1 for 24 rows. *Next row:* Change to C. Work Pat 1 for 24 rows. *Next row:* Change to D. Work Pat 1 for 20 rows. *Next row:* Bind off sts.

FINISHING: Sew back piece to front. **Border and Ties:** With No 4 needles and D, cast on 28 sts, pick up 74 sts along lower edge, cast on 28 sts at end of row. In Pat.1, K 2 rows. Change to C. K 2 rows. Change to B. K 1 row. *Next row:* Bind off sts loosely.

Envelope Sweater

Send this to your favorite one-year-old. The sweater uses the simplest of shapes, with the impact on the embroidered name, address, and stamp. It's particularly affordable, since you can make it with leftover yarn.

Size: 9 to 14 months.

Materials: Sport-weight wool yarn, 1.75 oz each light gray (MC) and red (CC). Knitting needles Nos 3 and 5. Crochet hook size C/2. Large-eyed embroidery needle. A few yards of fine white cotton. Light gray thread for embroidery, and sewing needle.

Pattern stitch: Pat 1: rib 1/1: *K 1, P 1, rep every row. Pat 2: St st: K 1 row, P 1 row.

Gauge: 19 sts = 4 inches = 26 rows (No 5 needles and Pat 2).

Finished measurements: Total length, 11 inches; chest, 18 inches.

BACK: With No 5 needles and CC, cast on 43 sts. Work Pat 1 for 1 inch (= 6 rows). *Next row:* Change to MC and Pat 2. Work until 9½ inches in total length. *Next row:* Change to CC and Pat 1. Work for 1 inch. *Next row:* Bind off sts loosely in ribbing.

FRONT: Work same as for back.

SLEEVES: With No 5 needles and CC, cast on 28 sts. In Pat 1 work for 1 inch. *Next row:* Change to MC and Pat 2. Inc 6 sts evenly spaced across row (= 34 sts). Work even until 7½ inches in total length. *Next row:* Change to CC. K across row. *Next row:* On wrong side of work, K across row. *Next row:* Bind off sts loosely.

FINISHING: Sew side seams, leaving 4 inches open on upper body for armholes. Sew sleeve seams, set in sleeves crossing front neck ribbing over back neck ribbing.

STAMP: With No 3 needles and white cotton, in Pat 2, work a 2-inch square. With crochet hook and MC, work a sc row along square edges. On knitted square, with gray thread and sewing needle, using duplicate stitch, embroider "1¢." Sew stamp on upper left side of front with invisible seam.

EMBROIDERY: With large-eyed needle and CC, on front of sweater, using duplicate st, embroider name of the loved one and perhaps initials of city or state. On back of sweater, starting at 4½ inches from lower edge using duplicate st, embroider a V-shaped back seam as of an envelope.

Home-Sweet-Home Bloomer

Your toddler will feel right at home in this fresh, 100 percent cotton bloomer. The little bell will charm the child as he or she makes the rounds. A great spring/summer outfit.

Size: 1 to 3 years.

Materials: 100 percent cotton worsted-weight yarn, 3.5 oz white (MC) and 1.75 oz red (CC). Knitting needles Nos 4, 5, and 6. Tiny black button, 1 small bell, 2 Velcro (R) buttons.

Pattern stitch: Pat 1: St st: K 1 row, P 1 row. Pat 2: rib 1/1: *K 1, P 1, rep from * across row. Pat 3: seed st: Row 1: *K 1, P 1, rep from * across row. Row 2: *P 1, K 1, rep from * across row. Rep rows 1 and 2. Pat 4: garter st: K every row.

Gauge: 19 sts = 4 inches = 24 rows (No 6 needles and Pat 1).

Finished measurements: Total length, 15 inches; waist, 14 inches in ribbing.

Starting at lower edge of one leg, with No 5 needles and CC, cast on 40 sts. Work Pat 2 for 1 inch (= 8 rows). *Next row:* Change to No 6 needles and MC. Work Pat 1. Inc 1 st on each side, every other row, 5 times. *At the same time,* inc 1 st on each side of the 20 center sts, 5 times (= 60 sts). *Next row:* Place sts on holder. Work second leg the same way. Join two legs tog on same needle, placing 2 sts in middle for crotch (= 122 sts). Work even in Pat 2 until 8½ inches in total length. **Waist shaping:**   Change to No 4 needles and Pat 2. *Next row:* Dec 36 sts evenly spaced across row (= 86 sts). Work even in Pat 2 for 1¼ inches (= 10 rows). *Next row:* Bind off 22 sts on each side (= back).

FRONT BIB: With MC, continue on 42 center sts. With No 4 needles and Pat 3, work even for 4 inches.

ROOF: Change to CC. Work Pat 3. *Next row:* Dec 1 st on each side, every other row, 6 times. *Next row:* Bind off rem sts loosely.

STRAP: With No 4 needles and CC, cast on 7 sts. Work Pat 3 for 14 inches. *Next row:* Bind off sts. Work second strap the same way.

WINDOW: With No 4 needles and CC, cast on 10 sts. Work Pat 1 for 12 rows. *Next row:* Bind off sts loosely.

·**DOOR:**   With No 4 needles and CC, cast on 12 sts. Work Pat 1 for 21 rows. *Next row:* Bind off sts loosely.

FINISHING: Sew leg and back seams. Sew straps on outer edges of roof. Cross straps on back side. Sew Velcro (R) buttons over straps ends and on inner edge of back ribbing. Sew door and window on front bib with invisible seam. Place and sew a button on door as knob. Attach bell over door.

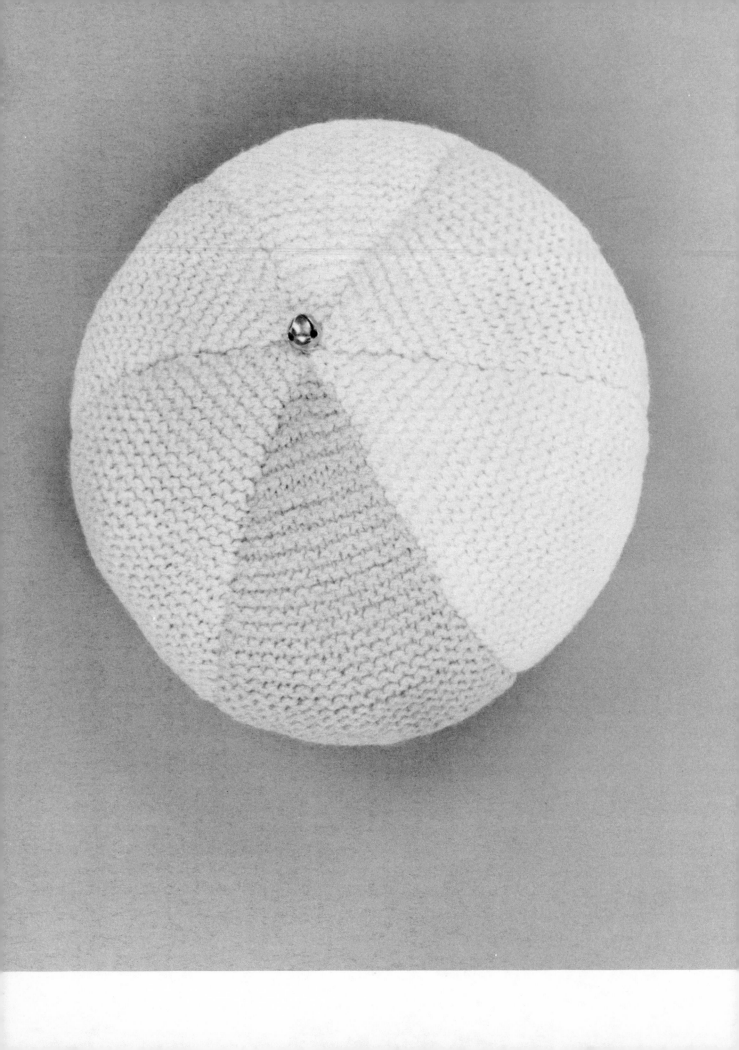

Balloon

Here's a quick and easy-to-do gift that uses leftover yarn.

Materials: Acrylic sport-weight yarn, 1 oz each blue, yellow, red, green, orange, pink, or any assorted colors. Knitting needles No 6. Polyester stuffing foam. Tiny bell.

Note: Pieces are worked in garter st: K every row. Follow chart to obtain right shape.

With No 6 needles, cast on 3 sts. Work garter st. *Next row:* Inc 1 st on each side, every other row, 5 times (= 13 sts). K 2 rows. *Next row:* Inc 1 st on each side, every 4 rows, 5 times (= 23 sts). Work even for 36 rows (= 18 ridges). *Next row:* Dec 1 st on each side, every 4 rows, 5 times (= 13 sts). K 2 rows. *Next row:* Dec 1 st on each side, every other row, 5 times. *Next row:* Bind off 3 rem sts. Work 5 separate pieces the same way.

FINISHING: Sew pieces together with invisible seam, leaving 1-inch opening on top for stuffing. Stuff balloon with polyester foam. Place and attach bell on top of balloon.

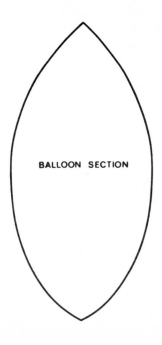

BALLOON SECTION

Elegant Doll

This very fine doll wears her own knitted outfit. She's not quick to make, but you know your daughter or grandchild will treasure her forever. A true heirloom.

Materials: 100 percent wool fingering-weight yarn. **Body:**   1 oz light pink or peach color (MC). **Clothes:**   1.5 oz green or contrasting color (CC). Knitting needles Nos 1 and 2. Stitch holders. Leftover of brown yarn or chenille (hair). Some blue and red cotton thread for eyes, face, and nails. Polyester stuffing. Four tiny buttons. Some leftover white yarn. Six inches of ½-inch-wide elastic. A pair of white nylon socks for doll.

Pattern stitch: Pat 1: St st: K 1 row, P 1 row. Pat 2: rib 1/1: *K 1, P 1, rep from * across row.

Gauge: 32 sts = 4 inches = 42 rows (No 1 needles and Pat 1).

Finished measurements (after stuffing):   Total length, 17 inches; arm with hand, 5 inches; leg with foot, 8 inches.

Note: The entire body is knitted in one piece except for arms, which are separate.

DOLL

BODY: Starting with head, with No 1 needles and MC, cast on 16 sts. Work Pat 1 for 4 rows. *Next row:* Inc 16 sts across row (= 32 sts). Work even for 4 rows. *Next row:* Inc 32 sts across row (= 64 sts). Work even until head measures 3 inches in total length.

NECK: *Next row:* K 2 sts tog across row (= 32 sts). Work even for 4 rows. *Next row:* K 2 sts tog across row (= 16 sts). Work even for 14 rows.

BUST: Divide work as follows: Place first 8 sts on holder. Continue work on rem 8 sts. **Bust front:**   Work in Pat 1 for 2 rows. *Next row:* Inc 20 sts across row (= 28 sts). Work even for 6 rows.

SHOULDERS: *Next row:* Inc 4 sts on each side (= 36 sts). Work even until bust measures 3½ inches in total length.

WAIST: *Next row:* Dec 4 sts in middle of work (= 32 sts). Work even for 2½ inches. Place rem sts on holder.

BACK: Work same as for front until back measures 6¼ inches in total length.

LEG: Each leg is worked separately. Take 16 sts from back and 16 sts from front. Work across first 32 sts. Place rem 32 sts on holder. **Leg shaping:** Dec 1 st on each side, every other row, 3 times (26 sts). Work even in Pat 1 until leg measures 6 inches in total length. **Foot shaping:** Dec 1 st on each side, every other row, until foot measures 1½ inches and 16 sts are left on needle. *Next row:* K 2 sts tog across row. *Next row:* Bind off sts. Work second leg the same way.

ARMS: With No 1 needles and MC, cast on 22 sts. In Pat 1 work even until arm measures 4 inches in total length. **Wrist shaping:** Dec 6 sts evenly spaced across row (= 16 sts). **Hand shaping:** Dec 1 st on each side, every 4 rows, twice (= 12 sts). *Next row:* K 2 sts tog across row. *Next row:* Bind off rem sts.

FINISHING: Sew foot, leg, and body side seams. Sew hand and arm seams. Sew shoulder and neck seams. Stuff doll firmly, giving shape to different parts of the body. Stuff head and sew head seam with invisible seam.

HAIR: Using brown yarn, cut strands 2 inches long. Cut loops 4 inches long. Sew loops on top of head. Sew strands across front of head (bangs).

EMBROIDERY: Using cotton thread, embroider eyes in blue. Embroider nose and mouth in red. On tip of each hand embroider tiny nails in red.

CARDIGAN

BACK: With No 2 needles and CC, cast on 34 sts. Work Pat 2 for 6 rows. Change to Pat 1. *Next row:* Inc 1 st on each side (= 36 sts). Work even for 2½ inches. **Armhole shaping:** At 3 inches of total length, bind off 2 sts at beg of next 2 rows twice. Work even in Pat 1 until back measures 5½ inches in total length. *Next row:* Bind off sts.

HALF FRONT: With No 2 needles and CC, cast on 18 sts. Work Pat 2 for 6 rows. Change to Pat 1. Work same as back until armhole measures 1¼ inches. **Neck-opening shaping:** Bind off 2 sts at beg of next 2 rows twice and dec 1 st at beg of next 2 rows once. At 5½ inches from beg, bind off rem sts. Repeat second half front the same way, reversing shaping.

SLEEVES: With No 2 needles and CC, cast on 30 sts. Work Pat 2 for 6 rows. Change to Pat 1. *Next row:* Inc 5 sts evenly spaced across row (= 35 sts). Work even until sleeve measures 3½ inches in total length. **Cap shaping:** Bind off 2 sts, on each side, every other row, 7 times. *Next row:* Bind off 7 rem sts. Rep a second sleeve the same way.

BUTTONHOLES BORDER: With No 2 needles and CC, cast on 4 sts. Work Pat 2, making 4 buttonholes of 2 sts evenly spaced on a total length of 4¼ inches. Bind off sts.

COLLAR: With No 2 needles and CC, cast on 44 sts. Work Pat 2 for 14 rows. *Next row:* Bind off loosely in ribbing.

FINISHING: Sew side and shoulder seams. Sew sleeve seams. Set in sleeves. Sew buttonholes border on right front edge. Sew collar around neck-opening edge. Sew buttons on left front edge facing buttonholes.

SKIRT

With No 2 needles and CC, cast on 34 sts. Work Pat 1 for 1½ inches. *Next row:* Inc 1 st on each side, every 6 rows, 9 times (= 52 sts). At 6½ inches of total length, K 4 rows. *Next row:* Bind off sts loosely. Repeat a second piece the same way.

FINISHING: Sew side seams. Fold waist. Sew with invisible seam, run elastic through, and fasten.

SCARF

With No 2 needles and white yarn, cast on 100 sts. Work Pat 1 for 22 rows. *Next row:* Bind off sts loosely.

Now, our doll is ready to be dressed!

Girl's School-Year Wardrobe

Red Dress

This versatile dress is perfect for every special occasion. The three-year-old can wear it below the knees with the sleeves rolled up; as she grows older it's worn shorter and the sleeves are let down.

Size: 3 to 5 years.

Materials: Wool/acrylic medium-weight yarn, 4 oz red (MC). Mohair/acrylic medium-weight yarn, 2 oz gray (CC). A few yards of Lurex metallic yarn, gold. Knitting needles No 4. Crochet hook size D/3.

Pattern stitch: Pat 1: garter st: K each row. Pat 2: St st: K 1 row, P 1 row. Pat 3: rib 1/1: *K 1 st, P 1 st, rep from * across row.

Gauge: 26 sts = 4 inches = 38 rows (No 4 needles and Pat 2).

Finished measurements: Total length, 18 inches; chest, 21 inches.

BACK: Starting at lower edge, in CC, cast on 130 sts. Work Pat 1 for 2½ inches. Change to Pat 2 and MC. Work for 7½ inches. **Waist:** Dec 64 sts evenly spaced across row (= 66 sts). Work Pat 3 for 1½ inches (= 16 rows). Change to Pat 2. *Next row:* Inc 10 sts evenly spaced across row (= 76 sts). Work even in Pat 2 until piece measures 13 inches in total length. **Armhole shaping:** Bind off 4 sts at beg of next 2 rows. Bind off 2 sts at beg of next 2 rows twice. Dec 1 st at beg of next 2 rows once. Work even until 17½ inches in total length. **Neck-opening shaping:** Work across first 17 sts, bind off 24 center sts, join new ball of yarn, and work last 17 sts across. *At each neck edge,* bind off 3 sts at beg of next 2 rows and 2 sts at beg of next 2 rows. *At the same time,* work **shoulder shaping:** Bind off 4 sts, every other row, 3 times.

FRONT: Work same as for back until waist. **Waist:** Work even in Pat 3 for 8 rows. *Next row,* Eyelet row: *K 6, yo, K 2 tog, rep from * across row. Continue work in Pat 3 for 7 more rows. Change to Pat 2. *Next row:* Inc 10 sts evenly spaced across row (= 76 sts). Work even in Pat 2 until piece measures 13 inches in total length. **Neck-opening shaping:** Work across first 19 sts, bind off 20 center sts, join new ball of yarn, and work last 19 sts across. Work both sides at once: *At each neck edge,* bind off 2 sts, every other row, twice. Dec 1 st, every other row, 3 times. Continue work even until 17½ inches in total length. **Shoulders shaping:** Bind off 4 sts at beg of next row. Bind off 5 sts at beg of next row twice.

SLEEVES: With CC, cast on 42 sts. Work Pat 1 for 1 inch. Change to Pat 2 and MC. Inc 1 st on each side, every 6 rows, 17 times (= 76 sts). Work even until sleeve measures 10½ inches in total length. **Cap shaping:** Bind off 4 sts at beg of next 2 rows. Bind off 3 sts at beg of next 2 rows. Bind off 2 sts at beg of next 2 rows. Dec 1 st on each side, every 4 rows, 4 times. Dec 1 st on each side, every other row, 6 times. Bind off 2 sts at beg of next 2 rows 4 times. Bind off rem 22 sts. Rep a second sleeve the same way.

COLLAR: With CC, cast on 130 sts. Work Pat 1 for 1¼ inches. Bind off sts loosely.

FINISHING: Sew side and sleeve seams. Set in sleeve, gathering fullness at sleeve cap. Place collar ½ inch on outer edge of neck opening. Sew with invisible seam.

BELT: Using double strand of CC and Lurex, work a 42-inch braid. Starting on center front, weave belt through eyelet row of waist, leaving back of waist loose. With crochet hook and Lurex, work sc around bottom edge, turn, work sl st on previous round. Work sc around collar edge, turn, sl st on previous round. Work sc around sleeve edge, turn, sl st on previous round.

Half-and-Half Dress

Use your imagination in combining fabric and yarn for this school-year outfit. There are hundreds of cotton prints to choose from, and it's fun to mix and match these with a favorite yarn. Use the instructions as a guide for making a unique garment.

Size: 3 to 5 years.
Materials: 100 percent wool shetland medium-weight yarn, 5 oz rose pink. Knitting needles Nos 4 and 5. Half a yard in any wide width of cotton print or Liberty. Twenty-four inches of ½-inch-wide elastic. Matching sewing thread.
Pattern stitch: Pat 1: garter st: K each row.
Gauge: 22 sts = 4 inches = 36 rows (No 5 needles and Pat 1).
Finished measurements: Total length, 22½ inches; chest, 23 inches.

SWEATER

BACK: With No 5 needles, cast on 63 sts. Work in Pat 1 for 4 inches. **Armhole shaping:** Bind off 3 sts at beg of next 2 rows. Bind off 2 sts at beg of next 2 rows. Dec 1 st at beg of next 2 rows twice (= 49 sts). Work even in Pat 1 for 4 inches. **Neck-opening shaping:** Work across first 18 sts, bind off 13 center sts, join new ball of yarn, work across rem 18 sts. *On each neck edge*, bind off 3 sts, every other row, twice. Dec 1 st once (= 11 sts). Work even in Pat 1 until 9¼ inches in total length. **Shoulders:** Bind off rem sts loosely.

FRONT: Work same way as for back until 7¼ inches in total length. **Neck-opening shaping:** Work across first 19 sts, bind off 11 center sts, join new ball of yarn, work across rem 19 sts. *On each neck edge*, bind off 3 sts. Bind off 2 sts. Dec 1 st, every other row, 3 times (= 11 sts). Work even in Pat 1 until 9¼ inches in total length. **Shoulders:** Bind off rem sts loosely.

SLEEVES: With No 5 needles, cast on 35 sts. In Pat 1 inc 1 st on each side, every 6 rows, 7 times (= 49 sts). Work even for 9½ inches. **Cap shaping:** Bind off 3 sts at beg of next 2 rows. Bind off 2 sts at beg of next 2 rows. Dec 1 st on each side, every other row, 6 times. Bind off 2 sts at beg of next 4 rows 3 times. Work even 2 more rows. Bind off rem 15 sts. Rep a second sleeve the same way.

NECKBAND: With No 4 needles, cast on 88 sts. Work in Pat 1 for 1 inch (= 4 ridges). Bind off sts loosely.

FINISHING: Sew side and shoulder seams. Sew sleeve seams. Set in sleeves. Sew edges of neckband. With seam placed at center back, sew neckband over neck edge with invisible seam. With leftover fabric, hem an appliqué, heart-shaped, on upper left of front.

SKIRT

Cut fabric in the middle. Sew edges tog on each side.

WAIST: Fold edge on inside of skirt, sew a 1-inch hem. Run elastic through. Sew ends securely. Place skirt on inner edge of sweater with seams on each side. Sew in place with invisible seam. Hem bottom of skirt to obtain 13 inches in total skirt length (or to desired length).

BRAIDED BELT: Using triple strand of yarn, braid a 32-inch-long belt. Cross ends on lower front edge of sweater. Sew in place with invisible seam.

Designer Coat

You don't need a million to make a child look like a rich kid. This designer coat, made of fancy bouclé yarn, does it all for the price of a few skeins. How proud a preschooler will feel wrapped in this luxurious creation. And despite the great look, the coat is surprisingly easy to make.

Size: 2 to 4 years.

Materials: Wool/acrylic multicolored bouclé yarn, bulky weight, 7 oz pink/purple (MC). Acrylic/alpaca medium-weight yarn, 2.5 oz light purple, and 100 percent wool medium-weight yarn, 1.75 oz dark purple. Knitting needles Nos 5 and 11. Crochet hook size K/10½. Stitch holders. Three medium-size snaps.

Pattern stitch: Pat 1: St st: *K 1 row, P 1 row, rep from * across row. Pat 2: garter st: K each row.

Gauge: 11 sts = 4 inches = 14 rows (No 11 needles and Pat 1).

Finished measurements: Total length, 18 inches; chest, 27 inches.

Note: MC is worked in single strand of bouclé. CC is worked with double strand of light purple and single strand of dark purple yarns.

BACK: Starting at lower edge, with No 11 needles and MC, cast on 46 sts. Work Pat 1 for 2 inches. Dec 1 st on each side every 1½ inches 4 times (= 38 sts). Work even until 12 inches in total length. **Armholes:** Bind off 5 sts at beg of next 2 rows. Work even 4 more rows. *Next row:* Change to CC and work in Pat 2 for 4½ inches. **Neck opening:** K first 9 sts, bind off 10 center sts, leave last 9 sts on holder. Continue each side separately. Work even in Pat 2 until back measures 17 inches in total length. **Shoulder:** Bind off 5 sts on shoulder edge once. Bind off 4 sts. Repeat same work for other side, reversing shoulder shaping.

RIGHT FRONT: With No 11 needles and Pat 1, cast on 27 sts. Work for 2 inches. Dec 1 st on each side every 3 inches twice (= 25 sts). Work even until 6 inches in total length. **Pocket:** *K first 7 sts, work next 10 sts in Pat 2 and CC. K rem 8 sts, rep from * for 6 rows. **Pocket opening:** Bind off 10 center sts. **Pocket lining:** With No 5 needles and single strand of light purple, cast on 20 sts. In Pat 1 work for 3½ inches. *Next row:* Bind off sts. *Continue work on all sts:* K 7, cast on 10 sts on bound-off sts of pocket opening, K 8. In Pat 1 work even until piece measures 12 inches in total length. **Armhole:** Bind off 4 sts on left side (= 21 sts). Work even 4 more rows. *Next row:* Change to CC. In Pat 2 work until piece measures 15 inches in total length. **Neck-opening shaping:** On right edge of work place 5 sts on holder, work across row. *Next row:* Place 2 sts on holder, work across row. *Next row:* Place 2 sts on holder, work across row. *Next row:* Place 1 st on holder, work across row. *Next row:* Place 1 st on holder, work across row (= 11 sts on holder). Work even until 17 inches in total length. **Shoulder:** Bind off 5 sts on left edge, every other row, twice.

LEFT FRONT: Work same way as for right front, reversing each shaping.

SLEEVES: With No 11 needles and Pat 1, cast on 24 sts. Work for 4 inches. *Next row:* Inc 1 st on each side. Work even until 7 inches in total length. *Next row:* Inc 1 st on each side (= 28 sts). Work even until 9 inches in total length. *Next row:* Bind off sts loosely. Rep a second sleeve the same way.

FINISHING: Sew side and shoulder seams. Sew sleeve seams, leaving 1 inch open on armhole edge to fit armhole shaping. Set in sleeves.

COLLAR: With No 11 needles, pick up 11 sts from holder (left front), 28 center sts (back), and rem 11 sts from second holder (right front; = 50 sts). In MC work Pat 2 for 18 rows (= 9 ridges). Bind off sts loosely.

EDGING: With crochet hook and CC, work sc around collar edge and along each front edge. Fold collar on outside. Sew snaps on inner edge of right front and on outer edge of left front. Sew pocket lining on inside. Sew pocket border on each side.

Sweater, Skirt, and Vest

ge. Judy Emery

im : 10/11/2013

: 10/3/2013
Location : Cambridge Public Library

: Fashion knitwear for children.
: 746.9 Kap
: 0001000108413
Branch : Canajoharie Library

: 518-677-3220;
: 910 King Rd
CAMBRIDGE
NY 12816

irls!" And little girls look gorgeous in soft pink and
n this outfit give a fashionable look either worn

worsted-weight yarn, 11$\frac{1}{5}$ oz rose. Knitting nee-
het hook size F/5. One button for collar (sweater).
ide elastic (skirt).

1/1: *K 1, P 1, rep from * across row. Pat 2: St st: K 1
er st: K each row.

ches = 20 sts (No 6 needles and Pat 2).

Sweater: total length, 13$\frac{1}{2}$ inches; chest, 22 inches.
ches; waist, 21 inches.

SWEATER

les and MC, cast on 55 sts. Work Pat 1 for 1$\frac{1}{2}$ inches.
and Pat 2. *Next row:* Inc 1 st on each side (= 57 sts).
l 8$\frac{1}{2}$ inches in total length. **Armhole shaping:** Bind
2 rows. *Next row:* Dec 1 st on each side, every other
Work even until armholes measure 1$\frac{1}{2}$ inches. **Neck-
ide work as follows: Work across first 23 sts, bind off
l ball of yarn and work across last 23 sts. Work even
re 4$\frac{1}{2}$ inches. **Shoulder shaping:** On shoulder edge,
bind off 8 sts, every other row, twice. *Next row:* Bind off rem 7 sts.

FRONT: Same work as far back until armholes measure 2 inches. **Neck-opening shaping:** Divide work as follows: Work across first 22 sts, bind off 3 center sts, use a second ball of yarn and work across last 22 sts. *On each neck edge,* dec 1 st, every other row, 6 times. Work until armholes measure same as back. **Shoulder shaping:** On shoulder edge, bind off 8 sts, every other row, twice.

SLEEVES: With No 5 needles, cast on 27 sts. Work Pat 1 for 1 inch. Change to No 6 needles and Pat 2, inc 7 sts evenly spaced across first row (= 34 sts). Inc 1 st on each side, every 8 rows, 6 times (= 46 sts). Work even in Pat 2 until sleeve measures 9 inches. **Cap shaping:** Bind off 3 sts at beg of next 2 rows.

Dec 1 st on each side, every 4 rows, 6 times. Bind off 2 sts, at beg of next 2 rows, twice. Bind off rem 20 sts. Rep a second sleeve the same way.

COLLAR: With No 5 needles, cast on 29 sts. Work Pat 3 for 6 rows. *Next row:* Inc 6 sts across row (= 35 sts). Work Pat 3 for 8 more rows. Bind off 2 sts at beg of next 2 rows. Bind off rem 31 sts. Repeat a second piece the same way.

FINISHING: Sew side and shoulder seams. Sew sleeve seams. Set in sleeves, gathering cap on top of shoulder. Sew collar halves along neck-opening edge. With crochet hook, work sc around back neck opening. Work a ch loop on upper right edge. Sew button on opposite side.

SKIRT

BACK: With No 5 needles, cast on 104 sts. Work Pat 3 for 1 inch. Change to No 6 needles. Work in Pat 2 until 9½ inches in total length. **Waist shaping:** *Row 1:* *K 4, K 2 tog, rep from * across row. *Row 2:* P. *Row 3:* *K 3, K 2 tog, rep from * across row. *Row 4:* P on rem sts. Work 2 more rows. Change to No 4 needles and Pat 3. Work for 16 rows (= 8 ridges). Bind off all sts loosely.

FRONT: Same work as back.

FINISHING: Sew side seams. Sew one side of ridged waist. Fold waist on inside skirt. Sew with invisible seam. Run elastic through and fasten.

VEST

Size: 3 to 4 years.

Materials: Mohair medium-weight yarn, 1.5 oz medium gray (MC) and 1 oz each purple (A), natural (B), pink (C), and fuchsia (D). Knitting needles Nos 6 and 7. Crochet hook size I/9. Stitch holders.

Pattern stitch: Pat 1: garter st: K each row. Pat 2: bias St st: *Row 1:* Inc 1 st at beg of row, work to last 3 sts, K 2 tog, work edge st. *Row 2:* P. Repeat these 2 rows.

Gauge: 18 sts = 4 inches = 32 rows (No 7 needles and Pat 1).

Finished measurements: Total length, 13½ inches; chest 23 inches.

Note: Jacket is knitted in one piece.

Starting at lower edge, with No 7 needles, cast on 110 sts. Work color pat as follows: 4 rows MC, 4 rows A, 4 rows B, 4 rows C, 4 rows MC, 4 rows D. Rep these 24 rows (= 12 ridges). Work for 8 inches (= 30 ridges). **Armholes:** Divide work as follows: K 28 first sts. Place rem sts on holder.

RIGHT FRONT: Work even in color pat until 11½ inches in total length. **Neck-opening shaping:** Bind off 3 sts. *Next row:* Bind off 2 sts, every other row, twice. *Next row:* Dec 1 st, every other row, twice. Work even in color pat until 13 inches in total length. **Shoulder:** Bind off 19 rem sts.

BACK: Take 54 following sts from holder. Work even in color pat until 13 inches in total length. Bind off all sts loosely.

LEFT FRONT: Take rem 28 sts from holder. Work same way as right front, reversing neck-opening shaping. **Armhole bias borders:** With No 6 needles and MC, cast on 11 sts. Work Pat 2 for 11 inches, or to armhole length. Bind off sts. Fold bias border. Sew in place with invisible seam.

TIES: With No 6 needles and A, cast on 55 sts. Work Pat 1 for 6 rows. Bind off loosely.

FINISHING: Sew shoulder seams. With crochet hook and A, work 62 sc along neck opening. Sew tie on each neck-opening edge. Sew bias on inner edge of armholes. **Front borders:** Sew ¾ inch hem on inner edge of each front. Steam lightly.

Boy's School-Year Wardrobe

School Coat

By knitting with big needles you can make a warm coat quickly. Don't worry about letting the child wear it to nursery school; the coat's strong because it's worked with four strands of yarn. Added touches include the big red buttons and "martingale" belt.

Size: 2 to 4 years.

Materials: Acrylic/wool, sport-weight yarn, 7 oz each red, green, and blue/gray. 2-ply bouclé, lightweight yarn, 2 oz gray. Mohair/acrylic, medium-weight yarn, 3.5 oz gray. Knitting needles No 13. Crochet hook size K/10½. Four 1½-inch-diameter buttons. Two 1-inch-diameter buttons.

Pattern stitch: Pat 1: St st: *K 1 row, P 1 row, repeat from *. Pat 2: garter st: K every row.

Gauge: 10 sts = 4 inches = 15 rows (No 13 needles and Pat 1).

Finished measurements: Total length, 19 inches; chest, 24 inches.

Note: MC is worked with 1 strand each red, green, blue/gray, and gray bouclé. CC is worked with 1 strand each red, green, and gray mohair.

BACK: In MC cast on 46 sts. Work Pat 2 for 8 rows (= 4 ridges). Change to Pat 1, dec 1 st on each side, every 2 inches, 6 times (= 34 sts). Work even until 13 inches in total length. **Armhole shaping:** Bind off 2 sts at beg of next 2 rows twice. Dec 1 st at beg of next 2 rows. Work even in Pat 1 for 5½ inches. **Shoulder shaping:** Bind off 4 sts at beg of next 2 rows twice. Bind off rem 8 sts loosely.

LEFT FRONT: In MC cast on 34 sts. Work Pat 2 for 8 rows. Change to Pat 1, dec 1 st on right edge, every 2 inches, 6 times (= 28 sts). Work even until 13 inches in total length. **Armhole shaping:** On right edge bind off 3 sts once. Bind off 2 sts once. Dec 1 st once. Work even in Pat 1 for 5 inches. **Neck-opening shaping:** On left edge bind off 6 sts once. Bind off 3 sts once. Bind off 2 sts twice. Dec 1 st once. **Shoulder shaping:** Same as for back.

RIGHT FRONT: Same work as for left front until 11 inches in total length. *First buttonholes row:* On right edge: K 2 sts, bind off 3 sts, K 6 sts, bind off 3 sts, K across. *Next row:* P. *Next row:* K 2 sts, cast on 3 sts on bound-off sts. K 6 sts, cast on 3 sts on bound-off sts, K across. Work even in Pat 1. Repeat a second buttonholes row at 4 inches from first. *At the same time* work Armhole

shaping: Work as for left front, reversing shaping. **Shoulder shaping:** Work as for left front.

SLEEVES: In CC cast on 23 sts. Work Pat 2 for 8 rows. Change to Pat 1. Inc 1 st on each side, every 2 inches, 3 times (= 29 sts). Work even until 9½ inches in total length. **Cap shaping:** Bind off 3 sts at beg of next 2 rows. Bind off 2 sts at beg of next 2 rows. Dec 1 st on each side, every other row, 5 times. Bind off rem 9 sts. Rep a second sleeve the same way.

COLLAR: In CC cast on 24 sts. Work Pat 1 for 6 rows. *Next row:* Dec 1 st on each side, every 2 rows, 4 times. *Next row:* Bind off rem 16 sts loosely.

MARTINGALE: In CC cast on 16 sts. Work Pat 1 for 2 rows. *Next row:* Inc 1 st on each side (= 18 sts). Work for 2 rows. *Next row:* Dec 1 st on each side. Work for 2 rows. *Next row:* K across row. *Next row:* Bind off rem 16 sts loosely.

FINISHING: Sew side, shoulder, and sleeve seams with flat seam. Set in sleeves. Sew buttons on left side opposite to buttonholes. Sew "martingale" on back, sewing 2 smaller buttons on each side. Sew collar around neck-opening edge. With crochet hook and right side facing, in CC work a sc around collar, along front opening edge, and along bottom edge. Block and steam lightly.

Two-Way Sleeveless

This pattern gives you two sweaters for the price of one, since front and back are interchangeable. The sweater is easy and inexpensive to knit.

Size: 2 to 3 years.

Materials: 100 percent wool sport-weight yarn, 2 oz navy blue (A), 2 oz green (B). Knitting needles No 8. Crochet hook size H/8.

Pattern stitch: Pat 1: garter st: K every row. Pat 2: St st: K 1 row, P 1 row.

Gauge: 16 sts = 4 inches = 22 rows (No 8 needles and Pat 2).

Finished measurements: Total length, 12 inches; chest, 19 inches.

BACK-FRONT: In A cast on 34 sts. Work Pat 1 for 8 rows (= 4 ridges). Change to Pat 2. Work even for 10 rows. Change to B and work for 4 rows. *Next row:* *K 1 A, K 1 B, rep from * across row. *Next row:* P in B. In B work St st for 2 rows. *Next row:* *K 1 B, K 1 A, rep from * across row. *Next row:* P in B. In B work St st even for 4 rows. Change to A. Work even for 12 rows. **Armhole shaping:** Bind off 4 sts at beg of next 2 rows (= 26 sts). Change to B. Work St st even for 4 rows. *Next row:* *K 2 B, K 2 A, rep from * across row. *Next row:* *P 2 B, P 2 A, rep from * across row. *Next row:* *K 2 A, K 2 B, rep from * across row. *Next row:* *P 2 A, P 2 B, rep from * across row. In B work for 4 rows. Change to A. Work for 4 rows. Change to Pat 1. Work for 4 rows (= 2 ridges).

STRAPS: K first 5 sts, bind off 16 center sts, using a second strand of yarn, K last 5 sts. Work on both straps at once. Work even in Pat 2 for 10 rows. *Next row:* On inside edge: K first 2 sts tog. Work even for 12 rows. *Next row:* K first 2 sts tog. Work even for 12 rows. *Next row:* K first 2 sts tog. Work even for 4 rows. Bind off last 2 sts.

Work other side of sweater the same way, reversing colors.

FINISHING: Sew side seams, with crochet hook, in matching color. Work sc along each armhole side to end of strap. Repeat for each side. Block, steam, and press straps flat. Tighten knots to desired length.

V-Neck Sleeveless

Few yarns can rival the look and feel of chenille. Here it's knitted into a rich-looking, geometric-pattern sleeveless that works well with jeans, corduroys, and "painter's pants." This sweater's sure to draw rave reviews!

Size: 2 to 3 years.

Materials: 100 percent viscose velour yarn, worsted weight, 2 oz wine color (MC), 1 oz each blue (A), green (B), and sand (C). Knitting needles Nos 5 and 6. Crochet hook size F/5.

Pattern stitch: Pat 1: rib 2/2; *K 2, P 2, rep from * across row. Pat 2: St st and jacquard.

Gauge: 18 sts = 4 inches = 26 rows (No 6 needles and Pat 2).

Finished measurements: Total length, 14 inches; chest, 21 inches.

Note: When working jacquard, change and carry colors loosely across wrong side from edge to edge. (See How-To Section on jacquard.)

BACK: With No 5 needles and MC, cast on 44 sts. Work Pat 1 for 1½ inches. Change to No 6 needles and A. K and inc 6 sts evenly spaced across row (= 50 sts). Work even in Pat 2 for 5 rows.

COLOR PATTERN I: *Row 1:* K 4 MC, *K 9 A, K 2 MC, rep from * across row, end K 9 A, K 4 MC. *Row 2:* P 5 MC, *P 7 A, P 4 MC, rep from * across row, end P 7 A, P 5 MC. *Row 3:* K 6 MC, *K 5 A, K 6 MC, rep from * across row, end K 5 A, K 6 MC. *Row 4:* P 7 MC, *P 3 A, P 8 MC, rep from * across row, end P 3 A, P 7 MC. *Row 5:* K 8 MC, *K 1 A, K 10 MC, rep from * across row, end K 1 A, K 8 MC. *Row 6:* P MC across. In MC work even in Pat 2 for 5 rows. Change to A. Work even in Pat 2 for 5 rows. Inc 1 st on last row (= 51 sts).

COLOR PATTERN II: *Row 1:* K 4 A, *K 13 B, K 2 A, rep from * across row, end K 13 B, K 4 A. *Row 2:* P 5 A, *P 11 B, P 4 A, rep from * across row, end P 11 B, P 5 A. *Row 3:* K 6 A, *K 9 B, K 6 A, rep from * across row, end K 9 B, K 6 A. *Row 4:* P 7 A, *P 7 B, P 8 A, rep from * across row, end P 7 B, P 7 A. *Row 5:* K 8 A, *K 5 B, K 10 A, rep from * across row, end K 5 B, K 8 A. *Row 6:* P 9 A, *P 3 B, P 12 A, rep from * across row, end P 3 B, P 9 A. *Row 7:* K 10 A, *K 1 B, K 14 A, rep from * across row, end K 1 B, K 10 A. *Row 8:* P A across. In A work even in Pat 2 for 6 rows. Change to B. Work even in Pat 2 for 6 rows. Inc 1 st on last row (= 52 sts).

COLOR PATTERN III: *Row 1:* K 5 B, K 19 C, K 4 B, K 19 C, K 5 B. *Row 2:* P 6 B, P 17 C, P 6 B, P 17 C, P 6 B. *At the same time* work **Armhole shaping:** Bind off 3 sts at beg of next 2 rows. Dec 1 st at beg of next 2 rows (= 44 sts). *Row 3:* K 4 B, K 15 C, K 8 B, K 15 C, K 7 B. *Row 4:* P 4 B, P 13 C, P 10 B, P 13 C, P 4 B. *Row 5:* K 5 B, K 11 C, K 12 B, K 11 C, K 5 B. *Row 6:* P 6 B, P 9 C, P 14 B, P 9 C, P 6 B. *Row 7:* K 7 B, K 7 C, K 16 B, K 7 C, K 7 B. *Row 8:* P 8 B, P 5 C, P 18 B, P 5 C, P 8 B. *Row 9:* K 9 B, K 3 C, K 20 B, K 3 C, K 9 B. *Row 10:* P 10 B, P 1 C, P 22 B, P 1 C, P 10 B. In B work in Pat 2 for 6 rows. Change to C and work in Pat 2 for 10 rows. Change to MC and work in Pat 2 for 6 rows. **Neck-opening shaping:** Work across first 13 sts, bind off 18 center sts, join a second ball of yarn, work across last 13 sts. Work on both shoulders at once for 4 more rows. Bind off sts loosely for each shoulder.

FRONT: Same work as for back until armholes. After working armhole shaping as for back, divide for neck opening as follows: Work across first 20 sts, bind off 4 center sts, join a second strand of yarn, work across last 20 sts. Work on both sides at once. Continue to work jacquard as for back. **V-Neck shaping:** Dec 1 st on each neck edge, every other row, 4 times. Dec 1 st on each neck edge, every 4 rows, 3 times. Work even in Pat 2 until armhole measures same as back. Bind off rem 13 sts loosely for each shoulder.

FINISHING: Sew side and shoulder seams.

EDGING: With crochet hook and MC, work sc around V-neck opening and around each armhole. Steam lightly.

Halloween Masquerade

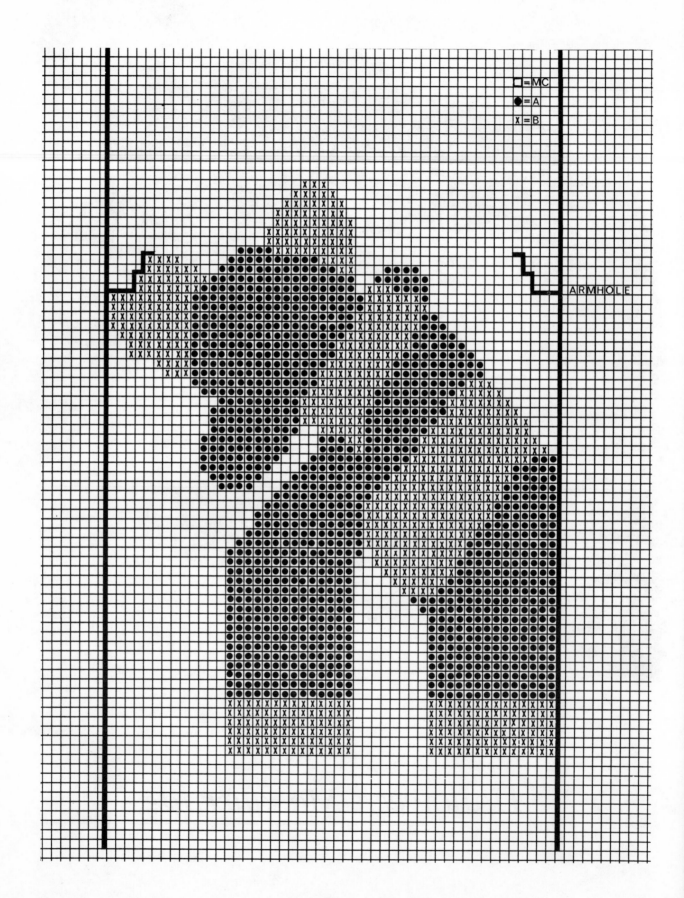

ARMHOLE

□=MC
●=A
x=B

58

Panda Bear Sweater and Earmuffs

Team up a five-year-old with this panda and you'll have an irresistible combination. The puffed sleeves give the sweater a fashionable look; the jacquard is easy to make. The earmuffs are a practical addition that no panda should do without.

Size: 4 to 5 years.

Materials: Acrylic/wool bouclé, heavyweight yarn, 8.75 oz red (MC), 1.75 oz each natural (A), black (B). Knitting needles Nos 4, 5, and 6. Crochet hook size F/5. Two 1-inch-diameter buttons. Large-eyed needle. Earmuffs band.

Pattern stitch: Pat 1: rib 1/1: *K 1, P 1, rep from * across row. Pat 2: St st and jacquard.

Gauge: 16 sts = 4 inches = 24 rows (No 5 needles and Pat 2).

Finished measurements: Total length, 15 inches; chest, 24 inches.

Note: Use a separate bobbin for each color change.

SWEATER

BACK: With No 4 needles and MC, cast on 42 sts. Work Pat 1 for 1½ inches. Change to No 5 needles and Pat 2. Inc 6 sts evenly spaced across row (= 48 sts). Work even until 10 inches in total length. **Armhole shaping:** Bind off 3 sts at beg of next 2 rows. Dec 1 st on each side, every other row, twice (= 38 sts). Work even in Pat 2 until armhole measures 4½ inches. **Neck opening:** Work across first 12 sts, bind off 14 center sts, join a second ball of yarn, work across last 12 sts, working both sides at once. **Shoulder shaping:** Bind off 6 sts, every other row, twice.

FRONT: Start work same as back until 2 inches in total length. *Next row:* Work jacquard pattern, following chart. Work armhole shaping as for back. Continue work even in Pat 2 until armhole measures 4 inches. **Neck opening:** Work across first 12 sts, bind off 14 center sts, join a second ball of yarn, work across last 12 sts. Work both sides at once. Work even for 4 rows. **Shoulder shaping:** Bind off 6 sts, every other row, twice.

SLEEVES: With No 4 needles and MC, cast on 24 sts. Work Pat 1 for 1½ inches. Change to No 5 needles and Pat 2. Inc 6 sts evenly across row (= 30 sts). Inc 1 st on each side, every 1½ inches, 4 times (= 38 sts). Work even until 10 inches in total length. **Cap shaping:** Bind off 3 sts at beg of next 2 rows. Dec 1 st on each side, every 4 rows, twice. Dec 1 st on each side, every 6 rows, 3 times. Work even in Pat 2 until cap measures 5 inches. Bind off rem 22 sts. Rep a second sleeve the same way.

FINISHING: Run in all yarn ends on wrong side of front. Sew side and sleeve seams. Sew shoulders tog, leaving ½ inch open on neck-opening edge. Set in -sleeve, gathering fullness of cap. With crochet hook and B, work sc along each neck edge of front and back. On each front shoulder edge, work a loop to close with button. Sew button on opposite shoulder. With large-eyed needle and B, embroider over front jacquard panda's knuckles, top of front leg, eyes, nose, and mouth.

EARMUFFS

With No 6 needles and B, cast on 10 sts. Work in Pat 2 for 4 rows. *Next row:* Inc 1 st on each side. Work even for 8 rows. Change to A. Work for 8 rows. *Next row:* Dec 1 st on each side. Work even for 4 rows. Bind off. Repeat a second piece. **Band:** With No 5 needles and MC, cast on 6 sts. Work in Pat 2 to fit to length of earmuff's band.

FINISHING: Sew red band to band with flat seam. Sew pieces on each ear with invisible seam.

Sun/Moon Pajamas and Hat

The sleepwear of the year! These comfortable and warm pajamas will enchant a child right to slumberland. Stories of the sun and moon provide a nice bedtime treat.

Size: 2 to 3 years.
Materials: Wool/acrylic medium-weight yarn, 3.5 oz each medium blue and bright yellow. Mohair lightweight yarn, 2 oz light blue and 2.5 oz orange. Knitting needles Nos 4 and 6. Stitch holders. One 16-inch yellow zipper.
Pattern stitch: Pat 1: rib 1/1: *K 1, P 1, rep from * across row. Pat 2: St st and jacquard.
Gauge: 23 sts = 4 inches = 30 rows (No 6 needles and Pat 2).
Finished measurements: Total length, 27 inches; chest, 25 inches.
Note: Back body is worked in medium blue and light blue. Front body is worked in yellow and orange.

PAJAMAS

FIRST LEG: Starting at back lower edge, with No 6 needles and medium blue, cast on 38 sts. In Pat 2 inc 1 st on each side, every 6 rows, twice (= 42 sts). Work even until 10 inches in total length. **Crotch shaping:** On inside edge bind off 4 sts. Work 2 rows. Dec 1 st. Work 6 rows. Place sts on holder.

SECOND LEG: Work same as for first leg, but do not remove sts from needle.

BODY BACK: Join 2 legs tog. Sl sts from holder on No 6 needle, inc 2 sts in middle (= 76 sts). Work even for 18 rows. *Next row:* Using double strand of light blue mohair, work jacquard pattern, following chart. Work until 21 inches in total length.

SLEEVE: Cast on 45 sts on each side (= 166 sts). Work in Pat 2 for 4½ inches. Bind off all sts loosely.

HALF FRONT: In yellow. Work leg same as for back until 10 inches in total length. **Crotch shaping:** On inside edge bind off 4 sts. Work 2 rows, dec 1 st. Work even for 12 rows. *Next row:* Using double strand of orange mohair, work jacquard pattern, following chart. Work until 21 inches in total length.

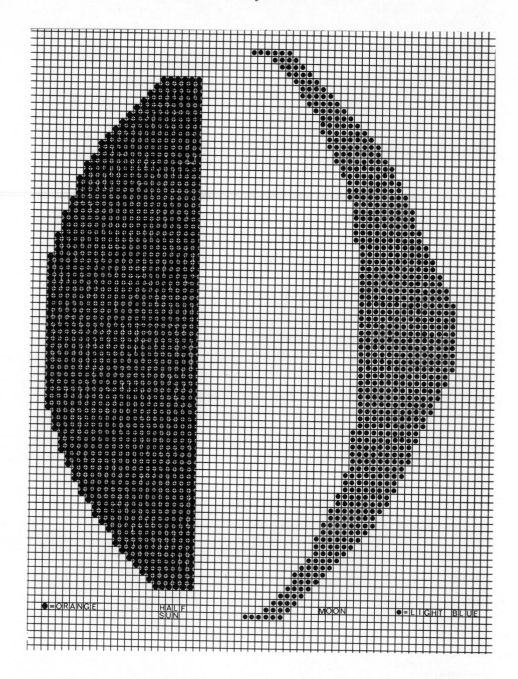

SLEEVE: On outside edge cast on 45 sts (= 82 sts). Work in Pat 2 for 4 inches. **Neck-opening shaping:** On neck edge bind off 6 sts. Bind off 3 sts, every other row, twice. Bind off rem 70 sts loosely. Work second half front the same way, but in reverse.

LEGBAND: Sew body side and leg side seams. With right side facing, using No 4 needles and single strand of orange mohair, pick up 56 sts along lower edge. Work Pat 1 for 1½ inches (= 12 rows). Bind off loosely in ribbing. Work the same way for second legband.

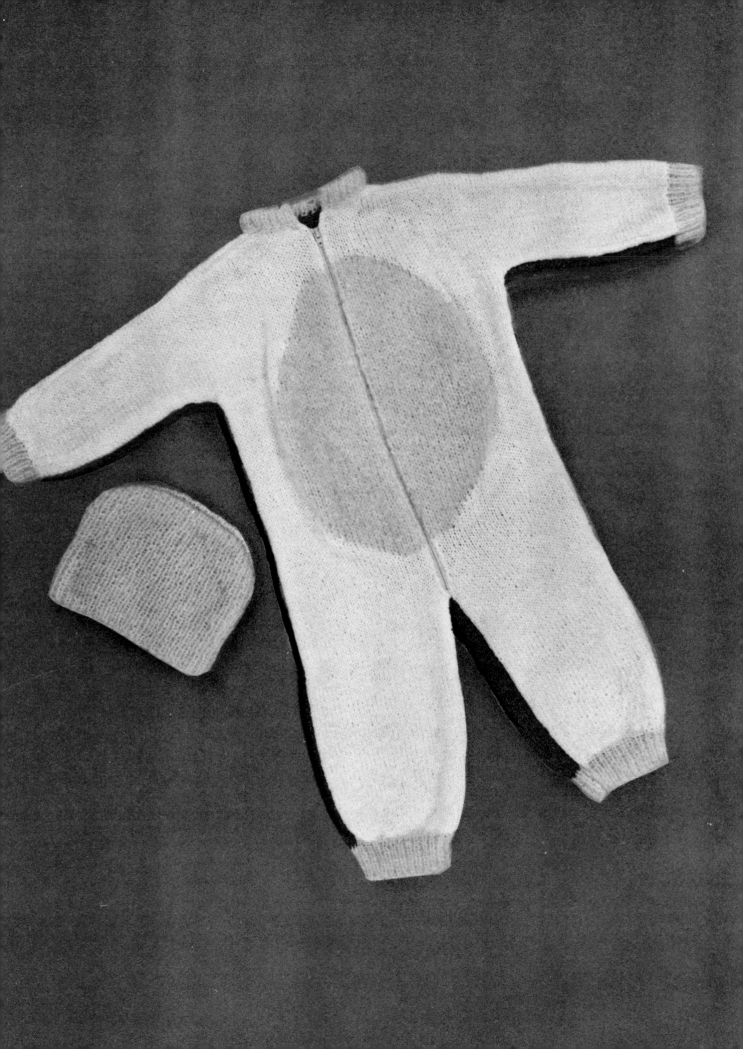

SLEEVEBAND: Sew shoulder and upperarm seams. With right side facing, using No 4 needles and single strand of orange mohair, pick up 42 sts along sleeve edge. Work Pat 1 for 1¼ inches (= 10 rows). Bind off loosely in ribbing. Work the same way for second sleeveband.

NECKBAND: With right side facing, using No 4 needles and single strand of orange mohair, pick up 60 sts along neck edge. Work Pat 1 for 1½ inches (= 12 rows). Bind off loosely in ribbing.

FINISHING: Sew leg and crotch seams. Sew legband with invisible seam. Sew underarm seams. Sew sleeveband with invisible seam. Fold neckband on outside and sew with invisible seam. Starting at neckband, sew zipper between front edges. Steam lightly.

HAT

FRONT: With No 4 needles, using single strand of orange mohair, cast on 50 sts. Work in Pat 1 for 5 inches. Bind off 4 sts at beg of next 2 rows. Bind off 3 sts at beg of next 2 rows. Bind off 2 sts at beg of next 2 rows. Bind off 4 sts at beg of next 4 rows. Bind off rem 20 sts loosely in ribbing.

BACK: Using single strand of light blue mohair, work same as front.

FINISHING: Sew middle and side seams with invisible stitches.

Jungle Suit and Cap

This is *the* outfit for monkeying around. The jungle design is a basic jacquard that I call "free jacquard" because you work it as you wish, changing the colors as desired. The kindergarten child will love wearing this at home and while visiting friends, and you know he'll be warm on those cold winter days.

Size: 4 to 5 years.
Materials: Acrylic/wool/mohair medium-weight yarn, 8.75 oz dark brown (MC), 7 oz yellow-orange (CC). Knitting needles Nos 4 and 5. Stitch holders.
Pattern stitch: Pat 1: St st and jacquard. Pat 2: rib 1/1: *K 1, P 1, rep from * across row. Pat 3: garter st: K every row.
Gauge: 21 sts = 4 inches = 24 rows (No 5 needles and Pat 1).
Finished measurements: Sweater: total length, 15 inches; chest, 26 inches. Pants: total length, 24 inches; waist, 23 inches.
Note: Free jacquard: Follow chart as a base but change color pattern with your own inspiration, keeping brown as MC and using CC only for spots. Carry color not being used loosely across wrong side from edge to edge, twisting colors every fourth stitch.

SWEATER

BACK: With No 4 needles and CC, cast on 56 sts. Work Pat 2 for 1½ inches. Change to No 5 needles and Pat 1. *Next row:* With MC, inc 10 sts evenly spaced across row (= 66 sts). P 1 row. Work even in free jacquard until piece measures 10 inches. **Armhole shaping:** Bind off 3 sts at beg of next 2 rows. Dec 1 st on each side, every other row, twice (= 56 sts). Continue work even in free jacquard until armhole measures 5 inches. **Neck opening:** With MC, work across first 18 sts, bind off 20 center sts; using a separate ball of yarn, work across last 18 sts. Working both sides at once, work even for 2 rows. **Shoulder shaping:** Bind off 9 sts, at the beg of next 2 rows, twice.

FRONT: Work same as back until armhole measures 4 inches. **Neck opening:** Work across first 20 sts, bind off 16 center sts, using a separate ball of yarn. Work across last 20 sts, working both sides at once. On neck edge dec 1 st, every 4 rows, twice. **Shoulder shaping:** Bind off 9 sts, at the beg of next 2 rows, twice.

SLEEVES: With No 4 needles and CC, cast on 34 sts. Work Pat 2 for 1½ inches. Change to No 5 needles and Pat 1. *Next row:* With MC, inc 8 sts evenly spaced across row (= 42 sts). P 1 row. Inc 1 st on each side, every 8 rows, 8 times (= 58 sts). Work in free jacquard until sleeve measures 10½ inches in total length. **Cap shaping:** Bind off 3 sts at beg of next 2 rows. Dec 1 st on each side, every other row, 3 times. Dec 1 st on each side, every 4 rows, twice. Dec 1 st on each side, every other row, 3 times. Bind off 2 sts, at beg of next 2 rows, twice. Bind off 4 sts at beg of next 2 rows. Bind off rem 18 sts, knitting sts 2 by 2, across row.

COLLAR: Sew 1 side and 1 shoulder seam. With No 4 needles and CC, starting from open shoulder edge, pick up 66 sts around neck edge. Work even in Pat 2 for 4 inches. Bind off sts loosely in ribbing.

FINISHING: Sew second side and shoulder seam. Sew sleeve seams. Set in sleeve, gathering extra fullness of cap. Sew collar seam with invisible seam.

PANTS

Start at the foot of one leg.

SOLE: With No 5 needles and CC, cast on 40 sts. Work Pat 1. Inc 1 st on each edge and on each side of 2 center sts, every other row, 5 times (= 60 sts). Work 2 rows. Change to Pat 3. Work even for 6 rows (= 3 ridges). *Next row:* Change to MC. Work even in Pat 3 for 10 rows (= 5 ridges).

TOP OF FOOT: Place 24 sts of each side on separate holders. In Pat 1 work on 12 center sts as follows: *Pick up 1 st from holders on each side and K with first and last st of 12 center sts, rep from * for 10 times. Work even for 4 rows.

ANKLE: In Pat 2 work even all 40 sts for 2 inches. Place sts on holder. Work second foot the same way.

LEG—Back part: Sl 20 sts of back ankle from holder to No 5 needles. In MC and Pat 2 inc 6 sts evenly spaced across row (= 26 sts). P 1 row. *Next row:* Start free jacquard. On inside edge of leg inc 1 st, every 4 rows, 22 times (= 48 sts). Work even for 13 inches. Place sts on holder. Work the same way for back part of second leg.

BODY BACK: Join 2 back parts of legs tog on same No 5 needle.

CROTCH: With MC, dec 6 sts evenly spaced across row. Continue work in free jacquard pattern at the same time: Dec 1 st on each side, every 10 rows, 8 times (= 74 sts). Work even for 7½ inches. *Next row:* Dec 4 sts evenly spaced across row. P 1 row. Place sts on holder.

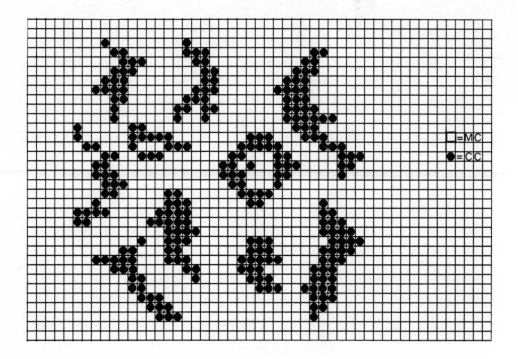

LEG—Front part: Sl 20 sts of front ankle from holder to No 5 needles. Work same as for back part until crotch. Work the same way for front part of second leg.

BODY FRONT: Join and work 2 front parts of legs the same way as for back body until 7½ inches from crotch.

WAIST: With No 4 needles and CC, join back and front tog on same needle. Work Pat 2 for 1½ inches. Bind off all 140 sts in ribbing.

FINISHING: Sew sole of foot. Sew back seam of ribbed ankle. Sew leg and crotch seams. Sew side seams. Sew waist seam with invisible seam. Steam lightly.

CAP

With No 5 needles and CC, cast on 70 sts. Work even in Pat 2 for 4 inches (or end of skein). Change to MC. Work even for 1 inch. *Next row:* In Pat 1: *K 2 tog, rep from * across row. P 1 row. *Next row:* *K 2 tog, K 4, rep from * across. row (= 29 sts). P 1 row. *Next row:* *K 2 tog, K 3, rep from * across row (= 23 sts). P 1 row. *Next row:* *K 2 tog, K 2, rep from * across row (= 16 sts). P 1 row. *Next row:* Sl yarn thread through 16 rem sts. Fasten securely on wrong side.

FINISHING: Weave middle seam.

Italian Harlequin Costume

A playful mohair costume for parties and holidays. The colors are becoming both for boys and girls of any complexion. The sweater is beautiful in itself when worn with pants or skirts.

Size: 4 to 5 years.

Materials: Mohair sport-weight yarn, 3.5 oz each, peach (A), purple (B), chestnut (C), and sky-blue (D). Knitting needles Nos 8, 10, and 10½. Crochet hook size G/6. Stitch holders.

Pattern stitch: Pat 1: rib 1/1: *K 1, P 1, rep from * across row. Pat 2: St st: *K 1 row, P 1 row. Pat 3: garter st: K every row.

Gauge: 14 sts = 4 inches = 19 rows (No 10 needles and Pat 2).

Finished measurements: Sweater: total length, 15 inches; chest, 24 inches. Pants: total length, 15 inches; waist, 21 inches.

SWEATER

Starting at lower edge of one sleeve with No 8 needles and A, cast on 32 sts. Work Pat 2 for 6 rows. Change to No 10 needles and Pat 3. Work for 8 rows (= 4 ridges). Change to C and Pat 2. Work for 6 rows. Change to Pat 3. Work for 8 rows. Change to B and Pat 2. Work for 6 rows. Change to Pat 3. Work for 8 rows. Change to D and Pat 2. Work for 6 rows. Change to Pat 3. Work for 4 rows until sleeve measures 9 inches in total length.

BODY: With D and Pat 3, cast on 28 sts on each side of sleeve (= 88 sts). Work even until 11½ inches in total length. **Neck-opening shaping:** Work across first 42 sts, bind off 4 center sts, place rem 42 sts on holder. Continue work on one side (= back or front). *On neck opening edge*, bind off 3 sts, K 1 row, bind off 2 sts, K 1 row (= 37 sts). Work even 2 more rows. *Next row.* Bind off all sts loosely. Repeat same work on rem 42 sts from holder. Work a second sleeve and half body the same way.

CENTER PIECE: Starting at lower edge, with No 10 needles and A, cast on 18 sts. Work in Pat 2 for 10 inches. *Next row:* Bind off sts loosely. Work a second piece the same way. **Neck border:** Sew center piece between each front and back body side. Sew one body side seam. With No 8 needles and C, pick up 62 sts around neck-opening edge. In Pat 1 work for 5 rows. *Next row:*

Bind off all sts loosely. **Sleeve border:** With No 8 needles and C, pick up 24 sts along sleeve edge. In Pat 1 work for 1 inch (= 6 rows). Using No 10 needles, bind off sts loosely in ribbing. **Sweater lower border:** With No 8 needles and C, pick up 60 sts around lower edge. In Pat 1 work even for 1½ inches (= 8 rows). With No 10 needles, bind off sts loosely in ribbing.

FINISHING: Sew second body side seam. Sew underarm seams. Weave all ribbing border seams. **Edging:** With crochet hook and C, around neck border, *3 sc, ch 3, sl st into last sc, rep from * for 1 round.

PANTS

Starting at lower edge of one leg, with No 10½ needles and B, cast on 52 sts. Work in Pat 2 for 20 rows. **Crotch shaping:** On inside edge bind off 3 sts. P 1 row. Place sts on holder. Work a second leg the same way. At 5½ inches in total length join 2 legs tog on same needle (= 98 sts). *Next row:* *K 2 first and 2 last sts tog, rep from * every 4 rows, 3 times. Work even in Pat 2 until 7 inches in total length. *Next row:* *K 2 tog, K 18, K 2 tog, K 50, K 2 tog, K 18, K 2 tog, * rep from * every 2 rows, once. Work even in Pat 2 until 9 inches in total length. *Next row:* Change to C and Pat 3. Dec 8 sts evenly spaced across row (= 74 sts). Work even for 8 rows (= 4 ridges).

WAIST BORDER: Change to No 8 needles and A. Still in Pat 3, dec 8 more sts evenly spaced across row (= 66 sts). In Pat 1 work even for 8 rows. Using No 10 needles, bind off sts loosely in ribbing.

LEG BORDER: With No 8 needles and C, pick up 30 sts around lower edge. In Pat 1 work for 8 rows. Using No 10 needles, bind off sts loosely in ribbing.

FINISHING: Sew back seams with flat seam. Sew underleg and crotch seams. Weave leg-border and waist-border seams.

Japanese Kimono

You can't give a child a more luxurious and comfortable bathrobe than this kimono. The characters on the back read "good luck," but even though they're Japanese, the knitting is easy to do! A wonderful birthday gift for a child of four to seven.

Size: 4 to 7 years.
Materials: 100 percent cotton velour sport-weight yarn, 8.75 oz red (MC) and 1.75 oz blue (CC). Knitting needles No 5. Crochet hook size F/5.
Pattern stitch: Pat 1: St st and jacquard.
Gauge: 16 sts = 4 inches = 24 rows.
Finished measurements: Total length, 23 inches; chest, 25 inches.

BACK: With No 5 needles and MC, cast on 58 sts. In Pat 1 work for 7 inches. *Next row:* Dec 1 st on each side (= 56 sts). Work even until piece measures 8 inches in total length. *Next row:* Joining CC, work jacquard pat, following chart. Work even until piece measures 16 inches in total length. **Armholes:** Cast on 5 sts on each side (= 66 sts). Continue work even for 6 inches or until back measures 22½ inches in total length. **Neck opening:** Work across first 25 sts, bind off 16 center sts, join new skein of MC, and work across last 25 sts. Work both sides at once for 4 more rows. Bind off sts loosely.

RIGHT FRONT: With No 5 needles and MC, cast on 36 sts. In Pat 1 work for 7 inches. *Next row:* Dec 1 st on left side. Work even for 4 inches. *Next row:* Dec 1 st on left side. Work even until piece measures 13½ inches in total length. **Opening shaping:** On opening edge bind off 2 sts. P 1 row. *Next row:* Dec 1 st, every 4 rows, 8 times, and dec 1 st, every 6 rows, 5 times. Work Pat 1 even until piece measures 16 inches in total length. **Armhole:** Work same as back. Continue work until right front measures 23 inches in total length. Bind off rem 24 sts loosely.

LEFT FRONT: Work same as right front, but reverse opening shaping.

SLEEVES: With No 5 needles and MC, cast on 18 sts. In Pat 1 work for 14 inches. Bind off sts loosely. Rep a second sleeve the same way. **Neck-opening border:** With No 5 needles and CC, cast on 5 sts. In Pat 1 work for 27 inches. Bind off loosely.

73

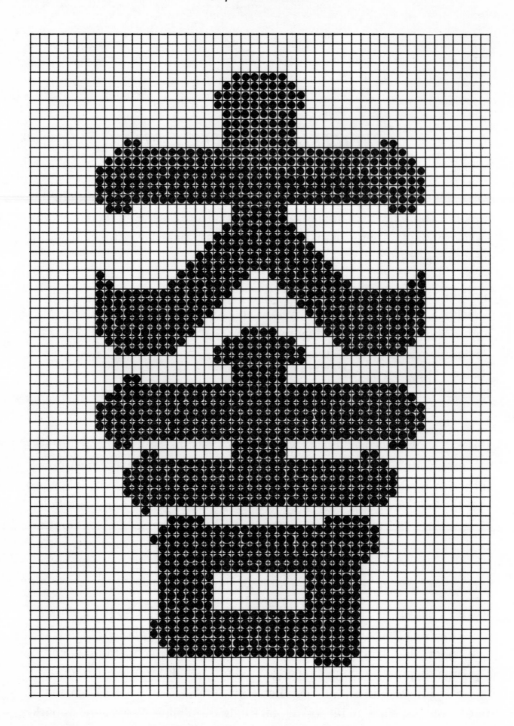

FINISHING: Sew body and upper sleeve seams. Set in sleeves. Sew border over neck-opening edge with invisible seam. On back, jacquard weave in ends of yarn. With crochet hook and CC, work a sc around lower edge of each sleeve.

TIE: With crochet hook and CC, work 2 ties of 30 chs each. Attach tie to front openings. Press kimono on wrong side under light steam.

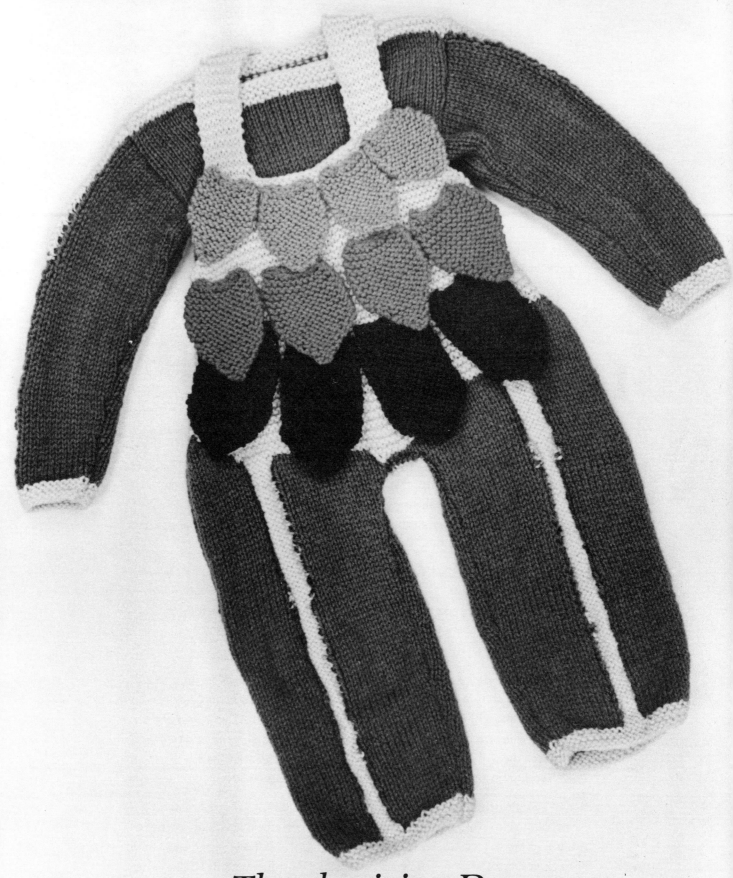

Thanksgiving Day

Turkey Overalls and Sweater

What makes the Great American Holiday so special? Why, family, friends, food—and fashion! The "turkey suit" will enhance the joy and fun of Thanksgiving Day for every child. The "feathers" on the bib are quickly knitted with leftover yarn. And on other days the sweater can be worn alone.

Size: 3 to 5 years.

Materials: Acrylic/wool worsted-weight yarn, 10.5 oz medium brown (MC) and 7 oz yellow (CC). Leftover yarns, ½ oz each red, orange, and dark red (or any other color) for feathers. Knitting needles Nos 6 and 7. Stitch holders. Two Velcro (R) square fasteners.

Pattern stitch: Pat 1: St st *K 1 row, P 1 row. Pat 2: garter st: K every row. Pat 3: St st in reverse.

Gauge: 17 sts = 4 inches = 23 rows (No 7 needles and Pat 1).

Finished measurements: Sweater: total length, 13½ inches; chest, 22 inches. Overalls: total length from waist, 21 inches; waist, 24 inches.

Note: Yellow stripes on sleeves and legs are worked in St st in reverse. On wrong side of work, cross strands of yarn loosely after each change of color.

SWEATER

BACK: With No 6 needles and CC, cast on 46 sts. In Pat 2 work for 6 rows (= 3 ridges). Change to No 7 needles and MC. In Pat 1 work for 12½ inches. *Next row:* Change to CC. In Pat 2 work for 6 rows. Bind off sts loosely.

FRONT: Work same as back until piece measures 11 inches in total length. **Neck-opening shaping:** Work across first 14 sts, place 18 center sts on holder, join new skein of MC, and work across last 14 sts. Work both sides at once. Place 1 st from each side onto holder with 18 center sts, repeat every 4 rows until piece measures 12½ inches in total length. *Next row:* Change to CC. In Pat 2 work even on all 46 sts for 6 rows. Bind off sts loosely.

SLEEVES: With No 6 needles and CC, cast on 26 sts. In Pat 2 work for 6 rows. Change to No 7 needles and MC. Inc 6 sts evenly spaced across row (= 32 sts). *At the same time* work 4 center sts in CC and Pat 3 (stripe). Inc 1 st on each side, every 1½ inches, 9 times (= 50 sts). Continue work in Pat 1 and Pat

3 until sleeve measures 8 inches in total length. *Next row:* On right side of work K 2 more sts in CC to middle stripe (= 6 center sts). Continue work until sleeve measures 12 inches in total length. Bind off all sts loosely. Rep a second sleeve the same way.

FINISHING: Sew side seams, leaving 5 inches open for armhole. Sew shoulder seams 2 inches from each armhole edge. Sew sleeve seams. Set in sleeves.

OVERALLS

BACK: Starting at lower edge of one leg, with No 6 needles and CC, cast on 24 sts. In Pat 2 work for 6 rows. Change to MC and Pat 1. *Next row:* Inc 6 sts evenly spaced across row (= 30 sts). *At the same time* work 4 center sts in CC and Pat 3 (stripe). Inc 1 st on each side, every 3 inches, 4 times (= 38 sts). Continue work in Pat 1 and Pat 3 until leg measures 10 inches in total length. *At the same time* on each leg and on right side of work, in Pat 2 and CC, inc 1 st on each outside edge of leg stripe. Rep every other row until back is all worked in CC and Pat 2. Work even for 2 inches. *Next row:* Dec 12 sts evenly spaced across row (= 48 sts). Work even for 1 inch. *Next row:* Dec 1 st on each side, every other row, 3 times. Work even until back measures 21 inches in total length. Bind off rem 42 sts (= waist).

FRONT: Same work as for back until front measures 21 inches in total length.

BIB: In Pat 2 and CC work on 42 sts. Dec 1 st on each side, every other row, 5 times (= 32 sts). Continue work even until bib measures 5 inches in total length from waist.

STRAP: K across 8 first sts, bind off 16 center sts. Place rem 8 sts on holder. Continue each strap separately. In Pat 2 work even for 14 inches. Bind off sts. Work second stripe the same way.

FINISHING: Sew side seams. Sew inside leg and crotch seams. Sew two Velcro (R) buttons on back waist of pants 6 inches apart and on each end of strap. Cross straps in back.

FEATHERS: 1. With No 6 needles and orange, cast on 2 sts. In Pat 2 inc 1 st on each side, every 4 rows, 4 times (= 10 sts). Work even for 14 rows. Bind off sts 2 by 2. Repeat 3 times. 2. With No 6 needles and red, cast on 2 sts. In Pat 2 inc 1 st on each side, every other row, 5 times (= 12 sts). Work even for 16 rows. Bind off sts 2 by 2. Repeat 3 times. 3. With No 6 needles and dark red, cast on 2 sts. In Pat 2 inc 1 st on each side, every other row, 5 times (= 12 sts). Work even for 20 rows. Bind off sts 2 by 2. Repeat 3 times. Sew feathers on front bib using back-stitch seam, placing lighter color on top row.

Cake Dress and Vest

This dress will get your daughter right into the spirit of the holidays. It's also, of course, a great birthday dress. The soft pastel colors compliment every complexion.

Size: 3 to 4 years.

Materials: Acrylic worsted-weight yarn, 2 oz each, medium blue (A), light pink (B), light blue (C), mint (D), and light yellow (E). Knitting needles Nos 5 and 6. Crochet hook size F/5. Some white cotton for edging and knitting candles (using a pair of matching needles). Orange thread for embroidery. A few yards of gold metallic thread. Large-eyed needle. Stitch holder.

Pattern stitch: Pat 1: garter st: K every row. Pat 2: St st: K 1 row, P 1 row.

Gauge: 21 sts = 4 inches = 20 rows (No 5 needles and Pat 1). 20 sts = 4 inches = 27 rows (No 6 needles and Pat 2).

Finished measurements: Dress: total length, 18 inches; chest, 18 inches. Vest: total length, 10 inches; chest, 21 inches.

DRESS

FRONT: With No 5 needles and A, cast on 78 sts. In Pat 1 work even for 2 inches (= 10 ridges). *Intermediate rows:* Change to No 6 needles. *Row 1:* *K 1, K 2 tog, rep from * across row. *Row 2:* P across row. Change to No 5 needles and B. *Row 3:* *K twice into next st, K 1, rep from * across row. *Row 4:* P across row. In Pat 1 work even for 2½ inches (= 13 ridges). *Intermediate rows:* Change to No 6 needles. *Row 1:* *K 1, K 2 tog, rep from * across row. *Row 2:* P across row. Change to No 5 needles and C. *Row 3:* *K twice into next st, K 1, rep from * across row. *Row 4:* P across row. In Pat 1 work even for 2½ inches (= 13 ridges). *Intermediate rows:* Change to No 6 needles. *Row 1:* *K 1, K 2 tog, rep from * across row. *Row 2:* P across row. Change to No 5 needles and D. *Row 3:* *K twice into next st, K 1, rep from * across row. *Row 4:* P across row. In Pat 1 work even for 2 inches (= 10 ridges). Change to Pat 2, work for 4 rows (= waist).

TOP: Change to No 6 needles and E. K 2 rows on all 48 sts. In Pat 2 work for 3 inches. **Armhole shaping:**   Bind off 3 sts at beg of next 2 rows. Bind off 2 sts at beg of next 2 rows. Dec 1 st at beg of next 2 rows (= 36 sts). Work even until top measures 4½ inches from waist. **Neck-opening shaping:** Work across first 17 sts, bind off 2 center sts, join new strand of yarn, and work across last 17 sts. *On each neck edge* bind off 2 sts twice, dec 1 st 3 times. Continue even until each shoulder measures 8 inches from waist. Bind off rem 10 sts.

BACK: Same work as front until top measures 6 inches from waist. **Neck-opening shaping:** Work across first 15 sts, bind off 6 center sts, join new strand of yarn, and work across last 15 sts. *On each neck edge* bind off 2 sts twice and dec 1 st once. Work 2 more rows. Bind off rem 10 sts.

FINISHING: Sew side and shoulder seams.

EDGING: With crochet hook and white cotton, work sc around lower edge of dress. Work sc around each armhole. **Neck opening:** Work sc around neck edge. **Picot edge:** *Next row:* *3 sc, ch 4, sl st into last sc, rep from * for 1 round.

CANDLES: With smaller needles and white cotton, cast on 5 sts (or any desired length). In Pat 2 work for 3 inches. Bind off. Repeat a second candle. Sew candles on top front with invisible seam. With orange thread embroider flame on top of candle.

BELT: With metallic thread used in double strand and crochet hook, work a round cord as follows: Work 4 chs, join them into a ring with sl st. Sl st into each st until cord measures 22 inches in total length. Sew belt around waist with invisible seam, crossing ends on center front.

VEST

Starting at lower edge, with No 5 needles and A, cast on 106 sts. In Pat 1 work for 2¼ inches (= 11 ridges). *Intermediate rows:* Change to No 6 needles. *Row 1:* *K 1, K 2 tog, rep from * across row. *Row 2:* P across row. Change to No 5 needles and B. *Row 3:* *K twice into next st, K 1, rep from * across row. *Row 4:* P across row. In Pat 1 work even for 2¼ inches (= 11 ridges). *Intermediate rows:* Change to No 6 needles. *Row 1:* *K 1, K 2 tog, rep from * across row. *Row 2:* P across row. Change to No 5 needles and C. **Armhole:** *Next row:* Divide work as follows. Work across first 27 sts (half front). Place rem 79 sts on holder. Continue work on second half front. *Row 3:* *K twice into next st, K 1, rep from * across row. *Row 4:* P across row. In Pat 1 work even for 2¼ inches (= 11 ridges). *Intermediate rows:* Change to No 6 needles. *Row 1:* *K 1, K 2 tog, rep from * across row. *Row 2:* P across row. Change to No 5 needles and D. *Row 3:* *K twice into next st, K 1, rep from * across row. *Row 4:* P across row. Work even in Pat 1 for 4 rows. **Neck-opening shaping:** On each neck edge bind off 3 sts, bind off 2 sts twice, and dec 1 st twice. Continue work even in Pat 1 and D for 2¼ inches (= 11 ridges). *Next row:* Bind off rem 18 sts loosely.

BACK: Place next 52 sts from holder on No 5 needles. Join C. Work even as for half front until last 2¼ inches (= 11 ridges) in Pat 1 and D. *Next row:* Bind off all 52 sts loosely.

SECOND HALF FRONT: Place rem 27 sts on No 5 needles. Join C. Work as for other half front, but reverse neck-opening shaping. After last 2¼ inches (= 11 ridges) in Pat 1 and D, bind off rem 18 sts loosely.

FINISHING: Sew shoulder seams.

EDGING: With crochet hook and white cotton, work sc around lower edge of vest and along front edge and neck edge. Work sc around each armhole.

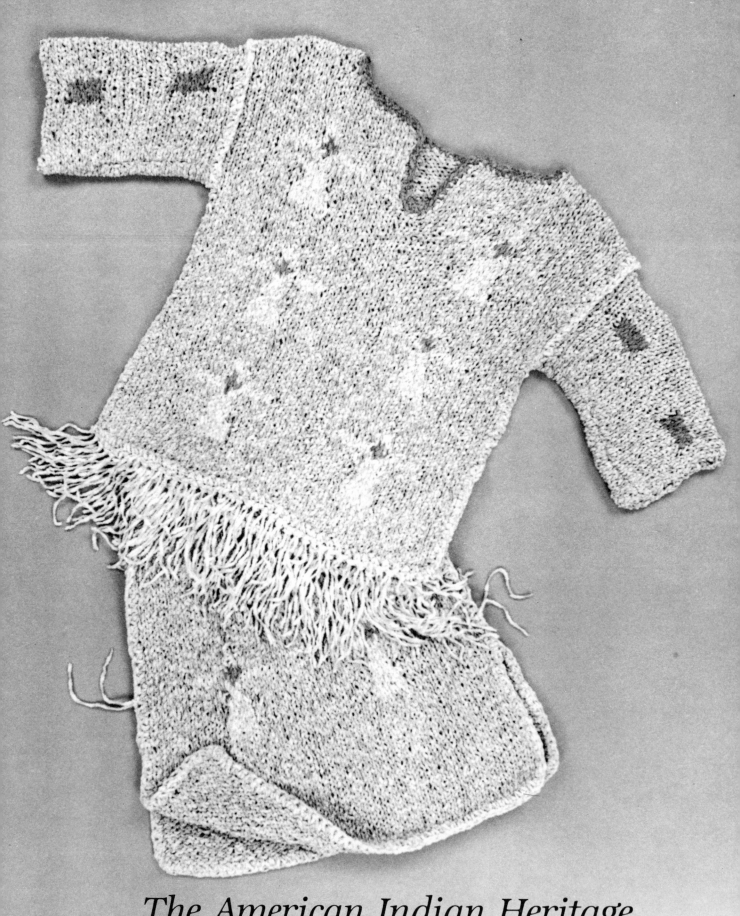

The American Indian Heritage

Indian Princess Tunic
and Skirt

This stunning outfit is based on an original American Indian design. It's made with velour, giving the tunic and skirt a rich, textured look. The three-year-old can wear the tunic alone as a dress; the set works for a girl of up to seven years old.

Size: 3 to 7 years.

Materials: 100 percent viscose velour worsted-weight yarn, 10 oz light blue (MC), 3 oz yellow (CC), and 1 oz pink (P). Knitting needles Nos 5 and 6. Crochet hook size F/5. 19 inches of 1-inch-wide elastic for waist.

Pattern stitch: Pat 1: St st and jacquard. Pat 2: garter st: K every row.

Gauge: 19 sts = 4 inches = 26 rows (No 6 needles and Pat 1).

Finished measurements: Tunic: total length, 15½ inches; chest, 21 inches. Skirt: total length, 13 inches; waist, 20 inches.

Note: When working jacquard pattern, use separate bobbins for each color. Cut and join color as needed. (See How-To Section.)

TUNIC

FRONT: With No 5 needles and MC, cast on 54 sts. K 2 rows. Change to No 6 needles. In Pat 1 work for 8 rows. *Next row:* Start jacquard pat. K11 MC, K7 CC, K18 MC, K7 CC, K11 MC. Work in pat following chart until piece measures 14 inches in total length. **Neck-opening shaping:**   Work across first 17 sts, bind off 20 center sts, join new ball of MC, and work across last 17 sts. On each neck edge dec 1 st. Work 2 more rows. *Next row:* Bind off rem 16 sts.

BACK: Work same as front until piece measures 11 inches in total length. **Back opening:**   *Divide work as follows:* Work across first 27 sts, join new ball of MC, and work across last 27 sts. Working both sides at once, work even until piece measures 13½ inches in total length. *On each neck edge* bind off 11 sts. Work even for 6 rows. *Next row:* Bind off rem 16 sts.

SLEEVES: With No 6 needles and MC, cast on 28 sts. K 2 rows. In Pat 1 work for 14 rows. **Color pattern:**   *Rows 1–3:* K 4 MC, K 6 P, K 8 MC, K 6 P, K 4 MC. *Rows 2–4:* P 4 MC, P 6 P, P 8 MC, P 6 P, P 8 MC. Continue work even for 22

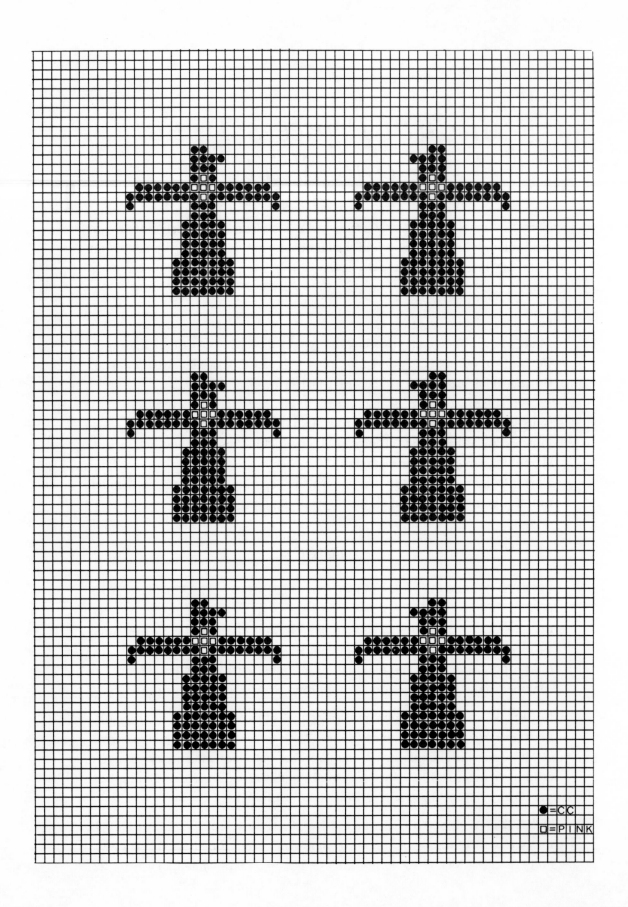

rows. Rep color pattern on next 4 rows. Continue work for 14 rows. Bind off rem 28 sts. Rep a second sleeve the same way.

FINISHING: Sew shoulder seams. Sew sleeve seam at underarm. Join sleeve and body tog on right side, placing center of sleeve to shoulder seam. With crochet hook and CC, work sc seam, leaving 4 inches open on lower side edge. On each back and front, work a row of sc along side and lower edge. Neck-opening edging: With crochet hook and P, work sc around neck edge for 1 round. In CC cut 2 ties 10 inches long. Place them on each side of opening.

FRINGES: In CC cut strands 7½ inches long. Knot each fringe in every other sc st of front and back lower edges. Trim ends evenly.

SKIRT

BACK/FRONT: With No 5 needles and MC, cast on 58 sts. K 2 rows. Change to No 6 needles. In Pat 1 work for 4½ inches. *Next row:* Start jacquard pat following chart. Work until piece measures 11½ inches in total length. *Next row:* Dec 1 st on each side (= 56 sts).

WAIST: Change to No 5 needles and CC. In Pat 2, work even for 10 rows. Bind off all sts.

FINISHING: With crochet hook and CC, join back and front tog on right side. Work sc seam, leaving 4 inches open on lower side edge. Work a row of sc along side and lower edge of each back and front. Sew elastic on inside waist, tightening elastic firmly on back side. In CC cut 2 ties 8 inches long. Place them on each side opening.

Midnight Dress

Here's a truly beautiful design for your daughter. The gold embroidery shimmers against the dark background. When worn with gold or white stockings, the effect is ravishing.

Size: 4 to 6 years.

Materials: Wool/acrylic worsted-weight yarn, 8.75 oz dark blue (MC), 1 oz gold Lurex. Knitting needles No 5. Large-eyed embroidery needle. Tiny turquoise beads, beading needle, and dark blue embroidery thread.

Pattern stitch: Pat 1: seed st. *Row 1:* *K 1, P 1, rep from * across row. *Row 2:* *P 1, K 1, rep from * across row. Repeat rows 1 and 2.

Gauge: 20 sts = 4 inches = 38 rows.

Finished measurements: Total length, 24 inches; chest, 26 inches.

Note: Embroidery pattern is given as a starting point. Following your own inspiration, you can add or change stitching pat as well as material.

BACK: Starting at lower edge, with No 5 needles and MC, cast on 90 sts. In Pat 1 dec 1 st on each side, every 12 rows, 12 times (= 66 sts). Work even until piece measures 16½ inches in total length. **Raglan shaping:**   Bind off 3 sts at beg of next 2 rows. Dec 1 st on each side, every other row, 7 times. Dec 1 st on each side, every 4 rows, 10 times. *Next row:* Bind off rem 26 sts.

FRONT: Work same as for back until piece measures 17½ inches in total length. **Front opening:**   Divide work as follows: Work across first 26 sts, join new ball of yarn, and work across last 26 sts. Work both sides at once. Continue working raglan shaping as for back until piece measures 23½ inches in total length. Bind off rem 13 sts.

SLEEVES: Cast on 64 sts. In Pat 1 work for 5 inches. **Raglan shaping:**   Bind off 3 sts at beg of next 2 rows. Dec 1 st on each side, every other row, 7 times. Dec 1 st on each side, every 4 rows, 10 times. Bind off rem 24 sts. Rep a second sleeve the same way.

FINISHING: Sew side and sleeve seams. Sew raglan seams.

EMBROIDERY: With large-eyed needle and gold Lurex thread, follow the chart. **Neck opening:**   At ¼ inch from neck edge, in stem st, work outline all around front and back. Work a second outline 1¾ inches apart from first

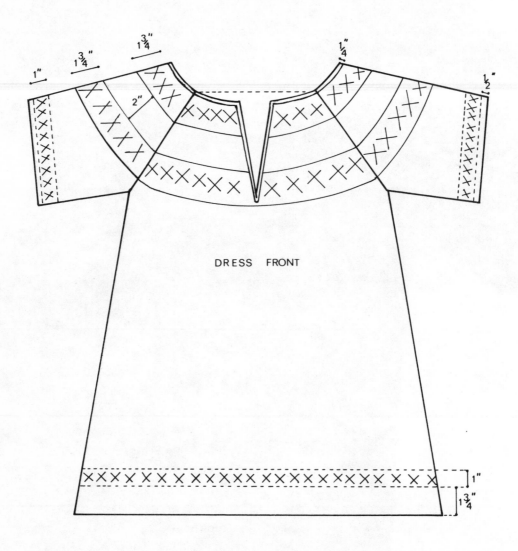

DRESS FRONT

outline. Work a third outline 2 inches apart from second outline. Work a fourth outline 1¾ inches apart from third outline (or just above first bound-off sts of raglan armholes). Between each first and second outlines, work a cross st row 1 inch high. With beading needle and dark blue thread, secure turquoise beads invisibly at each center cross. Repeat same work between third and fourth outlines. **Sleeves:** At ½ inch from sleeve edge, work a cross st row 1 inch high. **Lower body:** At 1¾ inches from lower edge, work a cross st row 1 inch high. Secure beads invisibly at each center cross.

Southwest Vest

This colorful vest will enliven your child's everyday wardrobe.

Size: 4 to 7 years.

Materials: Acrylic/wool worsted-weight yarn, 6 oz bright red (MC), 1.5 oz each french blue (A), bright yellow (B), and sand (C). Knitting needles Nos 6 and 7. Crochet hook size F/5.

Pattern stitch: Pat 1: garter st: K every row. Pat 2: St st and jacquard.

Gauge: 16 sts = 4 inches = 21 rows (No 7 needles and Pat 2).

Finished measurements: Total length, 16 inches; chest, 25 inches.

Pattern note: Use separate bobbins for each color pattern.

BACK: With No 7 needles and MC, cast on 52 sts. In Pat 2 work even for 4 rows. *Next row:* Join C and work Pat 1: *Row 1:* K 5 MC, *K 3 C, K 6 MC, rep from * across row, end K 3 C, K 8 MC. *Row 2:* P 8 MC, *P 3 C, P 6 MC, rep from * across row, end P 3 C, P 5 MC. *Row 3:* K 8 MC, *K 3 C, K 6 MC, rep from * across row, end K 3 C, K 5 MC. *Row 4:* P 5 MC, *P 3 C, P 6 MC, rep from * across row, end P 3 C, P 8 MC. Continue work even with MC for 4 rows. *Next row:* Join B and work Pat 2: *Row 1:* K 10 MC, *K 2 B, K 2 MC, K 2 B, K 2 MC, K 2 B, K 12 MC, rep from * across row, end K 2 B, K 10 MC. Continue pat, following chart until piece measures 9½ inches in total length. **Armhole shaping:** Bind off 2 sts at beg of next 2 rows. Dec 1 st on each side, every other row, twice (= 44 sts). Continue work even in Pat 2 until piece measures 13½ inches in total length. **Neck-opening shaping:** Work across first 14 sts, bind off 16 center sts, join new ball of MC, and work across last 14 sts. Work both sides at once. *At each neck edge* dec 1 st (= 13 sts). Work even for 8 rows. **Shoulder shaping:** Bind off 6 sts for each shoulder. Work even for 2 rows. Bind off rem 7 sts for each shoulder.

HALF FRONT: With No 7 needles and MC, cast on 29 sts. In Pat 2 work for 4 rows. *Next row:* Join C and work Pat 1: *Row 1:* K 2 MC, *K 3 C, K 6 MC, rep from * across row, end K 3 C, K 6 MC. *Row 2:* P 6 MC, *P 3 C, P 6 MC, rep from * across row, end P 3 C, P 2 MC. *Row 3:* K 5 MC, *K 3 C, K 6 MC, rep from * across row, end K 3 C, K 3 MC. *Row 4:* P 3 MC, *P 3 C, P 6 MC, rep from * across row, end P 3 C, P 5 MC. Continue work even with MC for 4 rows. *Next row:* Join B and work Pat 2: *Row 1:* K 8 MC, K 2 B, K 2 MC, K 2 B, K 2 MC, K 2

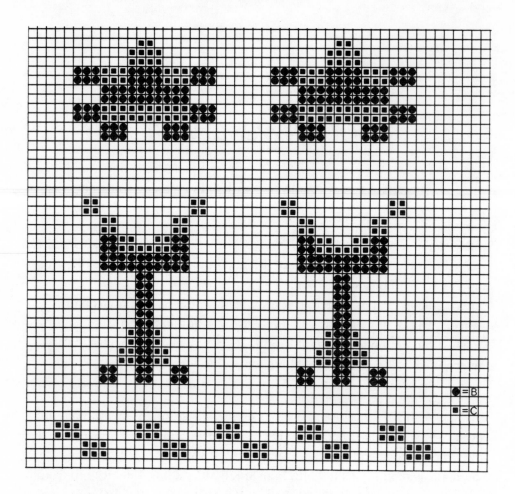

B, K 11 MC. Continue pat, following chart and working a single motif. Work even until piece measures 9½ inches in total length. **Armhole shaping:** Bind off 2 sts at beg of next row. Dec 1 st at beg of next row. Continue work even until piece measures 11 inches in total length. **Neck-opening shaping:** At neck edge dec 1 st, every other row, 13 times. *At the same time* work shoulder shaping as for back. Work second half front the same way to correspond to first half, reversing shaping.

FINISHING: Block pieces. Sew shoulder seams. **Armhole borders:** With No 6 needles and A, pick up 42 sts along armhole. K 4 rows. *Next row:* Change to MC. K 2 rows. *Next row:* Bind off sts loosely. **Bottom border:** Sew side seams. With No 6 needles and A, pick up 92 sts along lower body edge. K 4 rows. *Next row:* Change to MC. K 2 rows. *Next row:* Bind off sts loosely. **Neck-opening border:** With No 6 needles and A, pick up 84 sts along neck-opening edge. K 4 rows. *Next row:* Change to MC. K 2 rows. *Next row:* Bind off sts loosely. **Front side borders:** With No 6 needles and A, pick up 50 sts along front edge. K 4 rows. *Next row:* Change to MC. K 2 rows. *Next row:* Bind off sts loosely.

TIES: With crochet hook and B, ch 30. Fasten off. Repeat 3 more ties. Starting at each front neck-opening border, knot ties 3½ inches apart.

Scout Uniform

And for the family scout, here's a warm "hunting" outfit, again adapted from an American Indian design. It's comfortable to wear and perfect for playtime. The top and pants can be worn separately.

Size: 4 to 5 years.
Materials: Acrylic/wool worsted-weight yarn, 9 oz auburn (A), 2 oz each russet (B), walnut (C), toast (D), tangerine (E), orange (F), and apricot (G). Knitting needles No 7. Crochet hook size H/8. ¾ yard 1-inch-wide elastic for pants. Stitch holders.
Pattern stitch: Pat 1: garter st (K every row) and color pat.
Gauge: 16 sts = 4 inches = 32 rows (= 16 ridges). (No 7 needles and Pat 1).
Finished measurements: Tunic: total length, 14 inches; chest, 26 inches. Pants: total length, 22½ inches; waist, 21 inches.

TUNIC

Is worked in one piece and vertical color-stripe pat.

LEFT SLEEVE: Starting at lower edge of sleeve, with No 7 needles and G, cast on 34 sts. Work even in Pat 1 and color pat: With G, K 4 rows; with B, K 2 rows; with G, K 4 rows; with C, K 2 rows; with D, K 8 rows; with C, K 2 rows; with E, K 6 rows; with B, K 2 rows; with A, K 4 rows; with B, K 2 rows; with F, K 4 rows; with C, K 6 rows; with G, K 2 rows; with E, K 4 rows (= 52 rows). Rep same color-stripe pat and work for 7 inches.

BODY: With E, cast on 38 sts on each side of left sleeve (= 110 sts). Continue in color-stripe pat as for sleeve for 3 inches (shoulder). Neck opening: With E, K across first 52 sts (front), bind off 6 center sts, place last 52 sts on holder (back).

FRONT: Continue work in color-stripe pat and *at the same time* work Neck shaping: At neck edge dec 1 st, every 4 rows, 4 times (= 48 sts). Work even until last ridge with E (center of front). Rep the same work on other half front, reversing color-stripe pat and reversing shaping, increasing instead of decreasing for neck shaping. Work until first row with E. Place sts on holder.

BACK: Work same as for front until first row with E. *Next row:* Join front and back tog as follows: With E, K across first 52 sts from holder, cast on 6 center sts, and K across last 52 sts. Work even, reversing color-stripe pat, for 3 inches (shoulder).

RIGHT SLEEVE: With E, bind off 38 sts on each side of 34 center sts of sleeve. Work same as for left sleeve, reversing color-stripe pat. Work even until sleeve measures 7 inches in total length. With G, bind off rem sts loosely.

FINISHING: Sew body side and sleeve seams.

EDGING: With crochet hook and E, on right side of work, sc around neck-opening edge for 1 rnd, change to F, and rep a second rnd.

FRINGES: Following color-stripe pat, cut 6-inch strands of yarn in each color. With crochet hook, knot fringe in each st on lower edge of body and on underarm seam. Trim ends evenly.

PANTS

BACK: Starting at lower edge of one half leg, with No 7 needles and A, cast on 32 sts. In Pat 1 work even until piece measures 11 inches in total length. *Next row:* On inside edge dec 1 st (= 31 sts). Continue work even for 2 inches. Place sts on holder. Work a second half leg the same way. *Next row:* Join two pieces on same needle (= 62 sts). **Crotch shaping:** Bind off 2 sts in center of back, every 4 rows, 3 times (= 56 sts). In Pat 1 continue work even until piece measures 20 inches in total length. Place all sts on holder.

FRONT: Work same as for back.

WAIST: Join back and front tog on same needle (= 112 sts). On right side of work, work even in St st in reverse for 4 inches (P side on right side of work). Bind off sts.

FINISHING: Sew side, underleg, and crotch seams. Sew a 1¾-inch hem around waist. Run elastic through, adjusting to desired fit. Fasten off. Steam seam lightly on wrong side.

FRINGES: With A, cut 7-inch strands of yarn. With crochet hook, knot fringe in each st on lower edge of leg. Trim ends evenly.

Cruise Wear

Sailor Dress

Here's a great dress for every summer occasion. The sailor motif is stylish, and the look and feel are cotton-cool. She'll be ready to dance all night!

Size: 4 to 5 years.

Materials: 100 percent cotton bicolor slub lightweight yarn, 12 oz orange/natural (MC). Cotton/acrylic lightweight yarn, 1.75 oz natural (CC). Knitting needles Nos 3 and 4. Stitch holder.

Pattern stitch: Pat 1: St st: *K 1 row, P 1 row, rep from * across row. Pat 2: rib 1/1: *K 1, P 1, rep from * across every row.

Gauge: 24 sts = 4 inches = 32 rows (No 4 needles and Pat 1).

Finished measurements: Total length, 24 inches; chest, 23 inches.

BACK: With No 4 needles and MC, cast on 106 sts. In Pat 1 dec 1 st on each side, every 10 rows, 3 times. Continue work even until piece measures 15 inches in total length. Change to No 3 needles and Pat 2. *Next row:* Dec 22 sts evenly spaced across row (= 78 sts). Work even for 1½ inches. **Armhole shaping:**   Bind off 5 sts at beg of next 2 rows (= 68 sts). Continue work even in Pat 2 until piece measures 22 inches in total length. **Shoulder shaping:**   Bind off 5 sts at beg of next 2 rows 3 times. Bind off rem 38 sts.

FRONT: Work same as for back until armhole. **Armhole shaping:**   Bind off 5 sts at beg of next 2 rows (= 68 sts). *At the same time* divide front as follows: With No 3 needles and Pat 2, work across first 34 sts, join second ball of yarn and work across last 34 sts. Work both sides at once. **Opening shaping:**   *At each neck edge* dec 1 st, every 4 rows, 11 times. Continue work even until piece measures 22 inches in total length. **Shoulder shaping:**   Work same as for back. Bind off rem 8 sts for each shoulder.

SLEEVES: With No 3 needles and CC, cast on 60 sts. Work in Pat 2 for 1 inch. Change to No 4 needles and MC. In Pat 1 work even for 2 inches. **Cap shaping:**   Bind off 4 sts at beg of next 2 rows. Bind off 2 sts at beg of next 2 rows. Dec 1 st on each side, every 4 rows, 9 times (= 30 sts). Continue work even until sleeve measures 9 inches in total length. Bind off sts. Rep a second sleeve the same way.

COLLAR: With No 3 needles and CC, cast on 42 sts. In Pat 1, inc 1 st on each side, every other row, twice (= 46 sts). Work even for 3 inches. **Neck**

opening: Divide work as follows: Work across 10 first sts, bind off 26 center sts, join a second strand of yarn, and work across 10 last sts. Working both sides at once, at each inner edge dec 1 st, every 4 rows, 6 times. Then, at each outer edge, dec 1 st, every other row, 4 times. Fasten off. **Collarband:** With No 3 needles and CC, cast on 124 sts. In Pat 1 work 2 rows. *Next row:* Inc 1 st on each side, every other row, 5 times. Work even for 2 more rows. *Next row:* Change to MC. Work even for 4 rows. *Next row:* Change to CC. Dec 1 st on each side, every other row, 4 times. Bind off rem sts loosely.

FINISHING: Sew side, shoulder, and sleeve seams. Set in sleeve, gathering fullness at sleeve cap. Sew collarband to collar with invisible seam. Sew a ¼-inch hem around collar. Place collar along neck opening, sew with invisible seam. Steam seams lightly on wrong side.

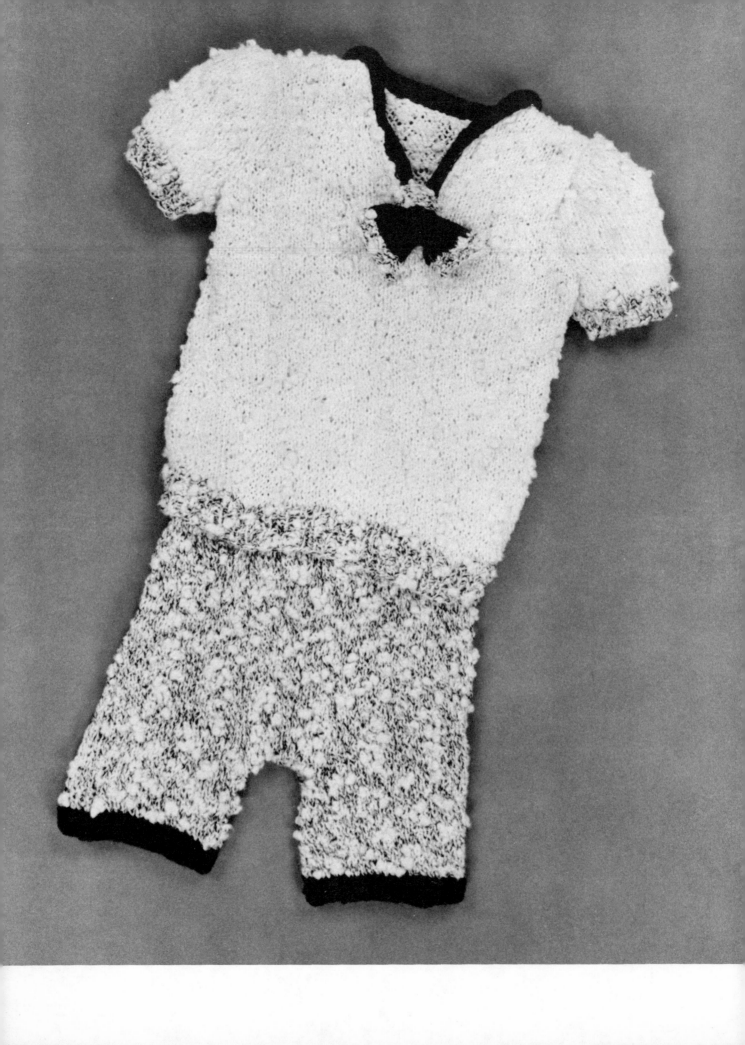

Polo and Shorts

"Anchors Aweigh!" With this outfit your child will feel right in step whether on the *QE2* or the nearest boardwalk. You know he'll be comfortable, too, since it's knitted in 100 percent cotton yarn.

Size: 2 to 3 years.

Materials: 100 percent cotton slub lightweight yarn, 4 oz natural (MC), 3 oz navy blue/natural (CC), 100 percent lightweight cotton yarn, 1.5 oz navy blue. Knitting needles Nos 3 and 4. Sixteen inches of 1-inch-wide elastic for shorts.

Pattern stitch: Pat 1: rib 1/1: *K 1, P 1, rep from * across every row. Pat 2: St st: *K 1 row, P 1 row, rep from * across row. Pat 3: garter st: K every row.

Gauge: 24 sts = 4 inches = 32 rows (No 4 needles and Pat 2).

Finished measurements: Polo: total length, 12 inches; chest, 22 inches. Shorts: total length, 11 inches; waist, 17 inches.

POLO

BACK: With No 3 needles and CC, cast on 46 sts. Work in Pat 1 for 1 inch. Change to No 4 needles and MC. In Pat 2, inc 10 sts evenly spaced across row (= 56 sts). Continue work even until piece measures 9½ inches in total length. **Armhole shaping:** Bind off 3 sts at beg of next 2 rows. Bind off 2 sts at beg of next 2 rows. Dec 1 st at beg of next 2 rows (= 44 sts). Work even until armholes measure 4 inches. **Neck-opening shaping:** K across first 13 sts, bind off 18 center sts, join a new ball of yarn, and K across last 13 sts, working both sides at once. Work for 4 rows. **Shoulder shaping:** At each shoulder edge, bind off 4 sts, at beg of next 2 rows, twice. Bind off rem 5 sts.

FRONT: Work same as for back until armholes measure ½ inch. **Neck-opening shaping:** K across first 23 sts, join a new ball of yarn, and K across last 23 sts, working both sides at once. *At each neck edge* dec 1 st, every other row, 10 times. Work until armhole measures 4 inches. **Shoulder shaping:** Work same as for back.

SLEEVES: With No 3 needles and CC, cast on 34 sts. Work in Pat 1 for 1 inch. Change to No 4 needles and MC. In Pat 2, inc 6 sts evenly spaced across row (= 40 sts). Continue work even until sleeve measures 1¾ inches in total length. **Cap shaping:** Bind off 3 sts at beg of next 2 rows. Bind off 2 sts at beg of next 2 rows. Dec 1 st at beg of next 2 rows, every other row, 3 times. Work even for 4 rows. Bind off rem 24 sts. Rep a second sleeve the same way.

COLLAR: With No 3 needles and navy blue, cast on 36 sts. In Pat 3 work for 4 rows. Change to Pat 2, work even for 4 inches. **Neck-opening shaping:**   K across first 6 sts, bind off 24 center sts, join a new strand of yarn, and K across last 6 sts. Working both sides at once, work even for 1 inch. *At each neck edge* dec 1 st, every 6 rows, 3 times. Work until piece measures 6 inches from neck opening. **Tie shaping:**   At each neck edge, and at the same time at each outer edge, inc 1 st, every other row, 6 times (= 15 sts). Work even for 4 rows. Change to Pat 3 and CC. Work even for 4 rows. Bind off sts loosely for each tie.

RING: With No 4 needles and CC, cast on 12 sts. In Pat 3 work for 4 rows. Bind off sts loosely.

FINISHING: Sew side and sleeve seams. Set in sleeve, gathering fullness at sleeve cap. Place collar along neck opening, sew with invisible seam. Sew end seam of ring, place around ties. Steam lightly.

SHORTS

BACK: With No 4 needles and CC, cast on 54 sts. In Pat 2 work even until piece measures 7½ inches in total length. **Crotch shaping:**   Work across first 24 sts, bind off 6 center sts, join a new ball of yarn, and work across last 24 sts. Work both legs at once in Pat 2 until piece measures 10½ inches in total length. **Leg border:**   Change to Pat 3 and navy blue. Work even for 6 rows. Bind off sts loosely.

FRONT: Work same as for back.

FINISHING: Sew side and underleg seams. Fold waist inside. Sew a 1-inch hem around waist. Run elastic through, adjusting to desired fit. Steam lightly.

Sweater with Boat

He may not win the America's Cup wearing this sweater, but he'll be the best-dressed crewman around. The boat and sun are made with a cross-stitch embroidery pattern that's easy to do when you follow the chart. What a pretty look!

Size: 2 to 3 years.

Materials: 100 percent fil d'Ecosse cotton lightweight yarn, 3.5 oz ecru (MC), 1.5 oz navy blue (CC). Knitting needles No 1. Three small buttons. Some blue, red, and yellow cotton thread for embroidery. Large-eyed tapestry needle.

Pattern stitch: Pat 1: rib 1/1: *K 1, P 1, rep from * across row. Pat 2: St st and stripes.

Gauge: 33 sts = 4 inches = 40 rows (No 1 needles and Pat 2).

Finished measurements: Total length, 12½ inches; chest, 19 inches.

BACK: With No 1 needles and MC, cast on 78 sts. Work in Pat 1 for 10 rows. Change to Pat 2, inc 1 st on each side (= 80 sts). Work even for 10 rows. *Next row:* Stripe pat: With CC, K 1 row, P 1 row. Change to MC. Work in Pat 2 for 14 rows. Rep these 16 rows for pat. Continue work even in stripe pat until piece measures 7½ inches in total length (6 rows after 4 CC stripes). **Armhole shaping:** Bind off 4 sts at beg of next 2 rows. Bind off 2 sts at beg of next 2 rows. Dec 1 st on each side, every other row, twice (= 64 sts). Work even in stripe pat until piece measures 12 inches in total length. After last CC stripe, work 2 more rows. Bind off sts loosely.

FRONT: Work same as for back until 10½ inches in total length. **Neck-opening shaping:** Work across first 27 sts, bind off 10 center sts, join new strand of MC, and work across last 27 sts, working both sides at once. *At each neck edge* dec 1 st, every 4 rows, 5 times (= 22 sts). Continue work even in stripe pat until armhole measures same as back. After last CC stripe, work 2 more rows. On right shoulder bind off rem sts loosely. On left shoulder, after last row, with MC, continue work in Pat 1. Work 2 rows. *Next row:* Work two buttonholes of 2 sts. *Next row:* Cast on 2 sts on bound-off sts. Work for 5 more rows. Bind off all sts in ribbing.

SLEEVES: With No 1 needles and MC, cast on 44 sts. Work in Pat 1 for 10 rows. Change to Pat 2 and stripe pat. Work for 4 rows. **Cap shaping:** Bind

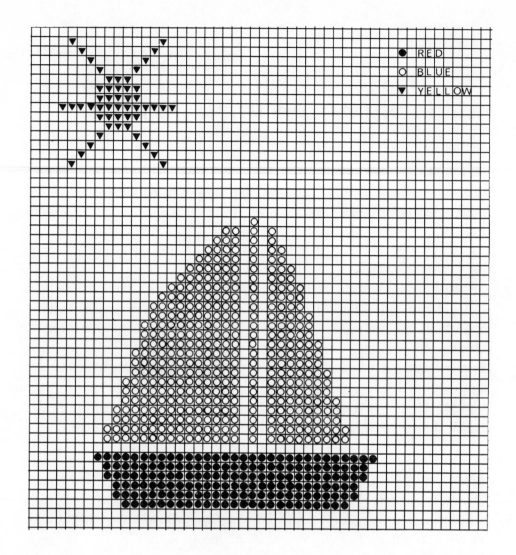

off 4 sts at beg of next 2 rows. Bind off 2 sts at beg of next 2 rows. Dec 1 st on each side, every 4 rows, 8 times. After second CC stripe, with MC work for 10 more rows. Bind off rem 16 sts. Rep a second sleeve the same way. **Neck-opening band:** Sew right shoulder seam. With No 1 needles and MC, starting at edge of left back shoulder, pick up 86 sts along neck edge. Work in Pat 1 for 2 rows. *Next row:* Work across until 6 sts from end of row. Work a buttonhole of 2 sts. *Next row:* After first 4 sts, cast on 2 sts on bound-off sts, work across. Work for 4 more rows. Bind off all sts loosely in ribbing.

FINISHING: Sew side and sleeve seams matching stripes. Set in sleeve, gathering fullness at sleeve cap. Sew buttons on back shoulder, facing buttonholes. Steam lightly.

EMBROIDERY: Following chart for boat, work in cross-stitch 28 sts from right side seam, starting 1 row over second CC stripe. Work sun in duplicate stitch for center circle and stem stitch for sun rays, starting 2 rows over fourth CC stripe.

Summer and Beach Clothes

Cape Cod Outfit

"Surf's Up!" This outfit, knitted in cool, 100 percent cotton, is perfect for those hot summer days. The hat is protective and fashionably floppy. The only accessories needed are a pail and shovel!

Size: 4 to 5 years.

Materials: 100 percent cotton worsted-weight yarn, 6 oz shocking pink (MC), 3 oz turquoise blue (A), and 3 oz white (B). Knitting needles Nos 5 and 6. Nineteen inches of ¾-inch-wide elastic for shorts.

Pattern stitch: Pat 1: garter st: K every row. Pat 2: basketweave stitch: *Rows 1 and 3:* *K 3, P 3, rep from * across row. *Rows 2 and 4:* *P 3, K 3, rep from * across row. *Rows 5 and 7:* *P 3, K 3, rep from * across row. *Rows 6 and 8:* *K 3, P 3, rep from * across row. Repeat rows 1 to 8. Pat 3: St st: K 1 row, P 1 row.

Gauge: 18 sts = 4 inches = 28 rows (No 5 needles and Pat 2). 16 sts = 4 inches = 32 rows (No 6 needles and Pat 1).

Finished measurements: Top: total length, 16 inches; chest, 24 inches. Shorts: total length, 9 inches; waist, 22 inches.

TOP

BACK: With No 5 needles and MC, cast on 54 sts. K 2 rows. *Next row:* Inc 1 st on each side (seam edge). In Pat 2 work even for 9½ inches. Change to No 6 needles and A. *Next row:* K 2 tog, K 52, K 2 tog. In Pat 1 K 3 more rows. **Armhole shaping:** Bind off 2 sts at beg of next 2 rows. Dec 1 st at beg of next 2 rows. K 2 rows. Dec 1 st on each side, every 4 rows, twice (= 44 sts). Work even in Pat 1 until piece measures 13 inches in total length. **Neck-opening shaping:** K across first 17 sts, bind off 10 center sts, join a new ball of yarn, and K across last 17 sts. Work both sides at once. *At each neck edge* dec 1 st, every other row, 5 times. Work even in Pat 1 until piece measures 15 inches in total length.

FRONT: Work same as for back until armholes measure 2½ inches. **Neck-opening shaping:** Work same as for back neck opening. Work even in Pat 1 until piece measures same as back. Bind off rem 12 sts for each shoulder.

FINISHING: Sew shoulder seams. Sew side seams, leaving 2½ inches open on each side lower edge.

SHORTS

Starting at lower edge of one leg, with No 6 needles and B, cast on 58 sts. In Pat 2 work even for 12 rows. Inc 1 st on each side, every other row, twice (= 62 sts). **Crotch shaping:** At each right edge of work (back side), bind off 3 sts, bind off 2 sts twice and dec 1 st twice. *At the same time,* at each left edge of work (front side), bind off 3 sts, bind off 2 sts, and dec 1 st twice (= 46 sts). Work even in Pat 1 until piece measures 8½ inches in total length. **Waist shaping:** Change to Pat 3. On left edge (front side), bind off 3 sts. P 1 row. *Next row:* On left edge, bind off 10 sts. K across. Work 2 more rows. *Next row:* On wrong side of work, bind off rem 33 sts. Work a second leg the same way, reversing crotch and waist shaping.

FINISHING: Sew front and back middle seams. Sew underleg and crotch seams. Fold waist border inside. Sew a 1-inch hem around waist. Run elastic through and fasten. Steam lightly.

HAT

Knitted in seven separate pieces.

TOP: With No 6 needles and MC, cast on 14 sts. In Pat 3 work for 12 rows. *Next row:* Dec 1 st on each side, every 4 rows, 5 times. Work 2 more rows. Bind off rem 4 sts. Repeat five similar pieces.

BORDER: With No 6 needles and A, cast on 10 sts. In Pat 1 K 5 rows. *Next row* (short row): K 5, turn, K back, K across all sts. Repeat this short row every 6 rows (after every third ridge). Work even for 208 rows (= 104 ridges). Bind off sts.

FINISHING: Sew pieces tog with invisible seam, using matching sewing thread. Sew end seam of border. With wrong side facing, sew border to lower edge of top hat with backstitch seam.

Gone Fishin' Outfit

Your little flapper will be the star of any beach from Malibu to the Riviera in this ensemble. The headband adds flair, and it will keep hair straight in even the stiffest sea breeze! What a way to hit the beach!

Size: 4 to 6 years.

Materials: 100 percent cotton worsted-weight yarn, 6 oz each white (MC) and turquoise blue (CC). Knitting needles Nos 5 and 6. Crochet hook size F/5. Twenty inches of ¾-inch-wide elastic for bermudas. One pair Velcro (R) buttons for headband.

Pattern stitch: Pat 1: St st and jacquard. Pat 2: garter st: K every row.

Gauge: 17 sts = 4 inches = 28 rows (No 6 needles and Pat 1).

Finished measurements: Top: total length, 17½ inches; chest, 24 inches. Bermudas: total length, 14 inches; waist, 23 inches.

TOP

BACK: With No 5 needles and CC, cast on 59 sts. In Pat 2 work for 8 rows. Change to No 6 needles and MC. In Pat 1 work for 8 rows. *Stripe:* Change to CC and work for 4 rows. Change to MC, work for 2 more rows. *Next row:* Start **First Jacquard Pattern:** *Row 1:* K 6 MC, *K 5 CC, K 9 MC, rep from * across row, end K 5 CC, K 7 MC. *Row 2:* P 4 MC, *P 8 CC, P 1 MC, P 1 CC, P 4 MC, rep from * across row, end P 8 CC, P 4 MC. *Row 3:* K 3 MC, *K 11 CC, K 3 MC, rep from * across row, end K 11 CC, K 3 MC. *Row 4:* P 4 MC, *P 8 CC, P 1 MC, P 1 CC, P 4 MC, rep from * across row, end P 1 CC, P 3 MC. *Row 5:* K 6 MC, *K 4 CC, K 1 MC, K 1 CC, K 8 MC, rep from * across row, end K 1 CC, K 5 MC. *Row 6:* P 6 MC, *P 4 CC, P 10 MC, rep from * across row, end P 4 CC, P 7 MC. *Next row:* With MC continue work even until piece measures 10 inches in total length. **Armhole shaping:** Bind off 3 sts at beg of next 2 rows. *Stripe:* Change to CC. *At the same time,* dec 1 st on each side, every other row, 3 times (= 47 sts). Change to MC. Work 2 more rows. *Next row:* Start **Second Jacquard Pattern:** *Row 1:* K 7 MC, *K 5 CC, K 9 MC, rep from * across row, end K 5 CC, K 7 MC. *Row 2:* P 5 MC, *P 8 CC, P 1 MC, P 1 CC, P 4 MC, rep from * across row, end P 1 CC, P 4 MC. *Row 3:* K 4 MC, *K 11 CC, K 3 MC, rep from * across row, end K 11 CC, K 4 MC. *Row 4:* P 5 MC, *P 8 CC, P 1 MC, P 1 CC, P 4 MC, rep from * across row, end P 1 CC, P 4 MC. *Row 5:* K 7 MC, *K 4 CC, K 1

MC, K 1 CC, K 8 MC, rep from * across row, end K 1 CC, K 6 MC. *Row 6:* P 7 MC, *P 4 CC, P 10 MC, rep from * across row, end P 4 CC, P 8 MC. *Next row:* With MC work even in Pat 2 until piece measures 13 inches in total length. **Neck-opening shaping:** K across first 18 sts, bind off 11 center sts, join new ball of yarn, and K across last 18 sts. Work both sides at once. *At each neck edge,* dec 1 st, every other row, 5 times. Work even for 4 more rows. Bind off rem 13 sts for each shoulder.

FRONT: Work same as for back.

FINISHING: Sew side and shoulder seams. With crochet hook and CC, work a row of sc around neck-opening edge.

BERMUDAS

Starting at lower edge of one leg, with No 6 needles and CC, cast on 60 sts. In Pat 1 work even for 3½ inches. *Next row:* Inc 1 st on each side, every other row, twice (= 64 sts). Continue work even until piece measures 4½ inches in total length. **Crotch shaping:** At each right edge of work (back side), bind off 3 sts, bind off 2 sts twice, and dec 1 st twice. *At the same time,* at each left edge of work (front side), bind off 3 sts and dec 1 st (= 51 sts). Continue to work even in Pat 1 until piece measures 12½ inches in total length. *Next row:* On right side of work, bind off 25 sts, K across. *Next row:* Bind off rem 26 sts. Work a second leg the same way, reversing crotch and waist shaping.

FINISHING: Sew front and back middle seams. Sew underleg and crotch seams. Fold and sew a 1-inch hem around waist. Run elastic through and fasten to desired fit. Steam lightly.

HEADBAND

With No 6 needles and CC, cast on 68 sts. K 2 rows. Work Pat 1 and inc 1 st on each side, every other row, 3 times (= 74 sts). *At the same time,* on the fifth row, work jacquard pattern as follows: *Row 1:* K 35 CC, K 5 MC, K 34 CC. *Row 2:* P 32 CC, P 8 MC, P 1 CC, P 1 MC, P 32 CC. *Row 3:* K 32 CC, K 11 MC, K 31 CC. *Row 4:* P 32 CC, P 8 MC, P 1 CC, P 1 MC, P 32 CC. *Row 5:* K 35 CC, K 4 MC, K 1 CC, K 1 MC, K 33 CC. *Row 6:* P 34 CC, P 4 MC, P 36 CC. With CC, work even in Pat 1 2 more rows. *Next row:* Dec 1 st on each side, every other row, 3 times (= 68 sts). Work even 2 more rows. Bind off sts loosely.

FINISHING: Sew Velcro (R) buttons on each end of headband. Steam lightly.

Hot-Pink Beach Robe

The perfect cover-up. Every child will feel glamorous in this robe made of spongy bouclé cotton. It's knitted in one piece, making for a quick and easy project. The robe is so soft and comfortable that you may end up knitting one just like it for yourself.

Size: 2 to 4 years.

Materials: 100 percent cotton eponge medium-weight yarn, 9 oz hot pink. Knitting needles No 4. Crochet hook size D/3. Stitch holders.

Pattern stitch: Pat 1: St st: K 1 row, P 1 row. Pat 2: garter st: K every row.

Gauge: 17 sts = 4 inches = 19 rows (No 4 needles and Pat 1).

Finished measurements: Total length, 19 inches; chest, 24 inches.

Note: Beach robe is knitted in one piece, starting at lower edge of back.

BACK: With No 4 needles and hot pink, cast on 66 sts. Work Pat 1, dec 1 st on each side, every 2½ inches, 6 times (= 54 sts). Continue work even until piece measures 14 inches in total length.

SLEEVES: Cast on 34 sts on each side of back (= 122 sts). Work even until armholes measure 4 inches. **Neck-opening shaping:**   K across first 51 sts (left front), bind off 20 center sts, place last 51 sts on holder (right front).

LEFT FRONT: On neck edge dec 1 st (= 50 sts). Work even for 1½ inches. **Front-opening shaping:**   At 2 sts from edge, inc 1 st, every 6 rows, 17 times. *At the same time,* when sleeve measures 8½ inches in total length, bind off 34 sts of sleeve. Work even in Pat 1 on rem sts until front piece measures 14 inches from armhole. *Next row:* Bind off rem 33 sts.

RIGHT FRONT: Work same as for left front, reversing shaping. **Opening border:**   With No 4 needles, starting in middle of back neck-opening edge, pick up 84 sts along neck and front edge. In Pat 2 work even for 8 rows. Next row work half collar: *Row 1* (short row): K 36, turn, K back. *Row 2* (short row): K 32, turn, K back. *Row 3:* K 44 sts. *Row 4:* Bind off sts loosely. Work second border and half collar the same way.

BELT: With crochet hook, ch 176 sts. Work a row of sc along chain. Fasten off.

FINISHING: Sew side and underarm seams. With crochet hook, work sc around bottom edge and around sleeve edge. Press under steam lightly.

New Clothes from Old

Jeans Culotte and Hat

Don't throw out your family's old blue jeans! Transform them into a practical and fun outfit. The bells on the shoulders and hat will bring smiles to the preschooler. And the low cost of making "new clothes from old" will cheer you.

Size: 2 to 4 years.

Materials: Acrylic sport-weight yarn, 2 oz natural. Knitting needles Nos 6 and 8: Crochet hook size H/8. Stitch holder. Five round medium-size bells as buttons. An old pair of jeans in adult size and matching sewing thread.

Pattern stitch: Pat 1: rib 1/1: *K 1, P 1, rep * across row. Pat 2: St st with garter ridge: *Rows 1 and 3:* K across. *Row 2:* P across. *Row 4:* K on wrong side of work. Repeat rows 1 to 4.

Gauge: 16 sts = 4 inches = 24 rows (No 8 needles and Pat 2).

Finished measurements: Total length, 23½ inches; chest, 20 inches.

TOP

BACK: Starting at lower edge, with No 6 needles, cast on 46 sts. In Pat 1 work for 1½ inches (= 10 rows). Change to No 8 needles and Pat 2. Inc 1 st at beg of next 2 rows (= 48 sts). Work even in Pat 2 until piece measures 5 inches in total length. **Armhole shaping:** Bind off 3 sts at beg of next 2 rows. Bind off 2 sts at beg of next 2 rows. Dec 1 st at beg of next 2 rows (= 36 sts). Continue work even in Pat 2 until armholes measure 3½ inches. **Neck-opening shaping:** Work across first 13 sts, bind off 10 center sts, place rem last 13 sts on holder. Continue work on one side. *At each neck edge,* dec 1 st twice. Work even in Pat 2 for 8 rows. Dec 1 st at beg of next row. Work even until piece measures 10 inches in total length. **Shoulder:** Bind off rem 10 sts. Work other side the same way, reversing neck-opening shaping.

FRONT: Work same as back until armhole measures 2½ inches. Work neck-opening shaping as for back.

FINISHING: Sew side seams. With crochet hook, work sc around neck-opening edge and around each armhole edge. **Shoulder edging:** Work a row of sc along each shoulder edge. On each front shoulder edge work two loops to close with bells. Sew bells on opposite shoulders. **Leg border:** With No 6

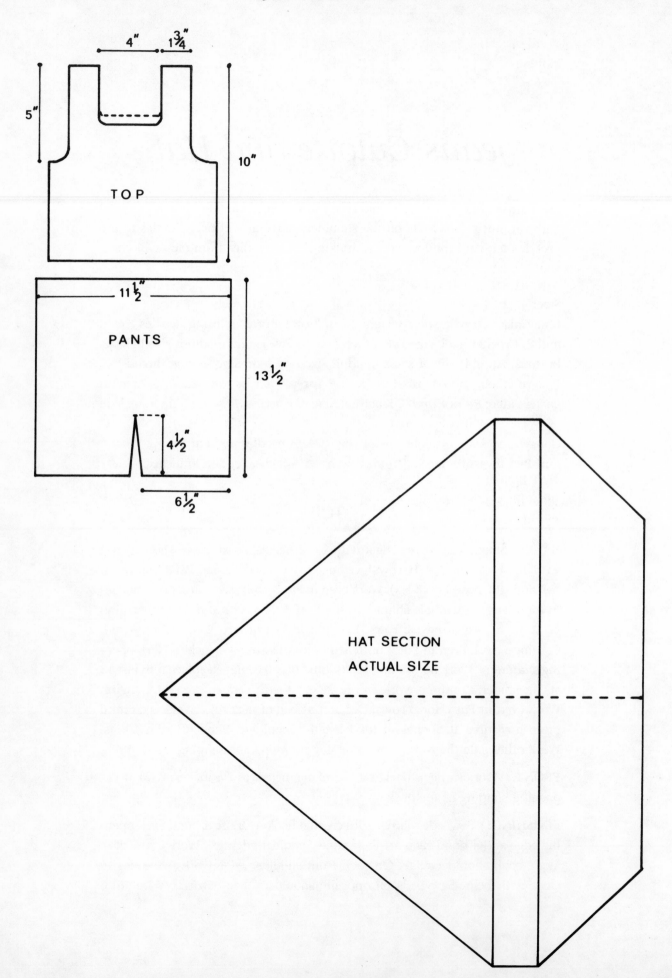

needles, cast on 52 sts. In Pat 1 work even for 1½ inches. Bind off sts loosely in ribbing.

CULOTTE

Following chart, enlarge to actual measurements. Draw pattern on wrong side of fabric, leaving ½-inch seam allowance. Cut two pieces for front and back. Cut a 2-inch square for crotch. With right sides facing, stitch front and back sides tog.

CROTCH: Place 2-inch square diagonally between legs, stitch edges. Sew hem at waist and at lower edge of each leg.

FINISHING: Lap knitted top over pants, sew in place with invisible seam. Stretch and sew leg border to each leg.

HAT

Following actual-size pattern lines, trace pattern on wrong side of fabric. Cut out five similar sections with an extra ¼-inch seam allowance. With right side facing, mark fold section of each piece, stitch sections tog starting at top seam. Trim seam at tip of hat and sew fifth bell over.

HAT BORDER: With No 6 needles, cast on 78 sts. In Pat 1 work even for ½-inch. Bind off sts loosely in ribbing. Stretch and sew hat border to lower edge of hat. Block pieces.

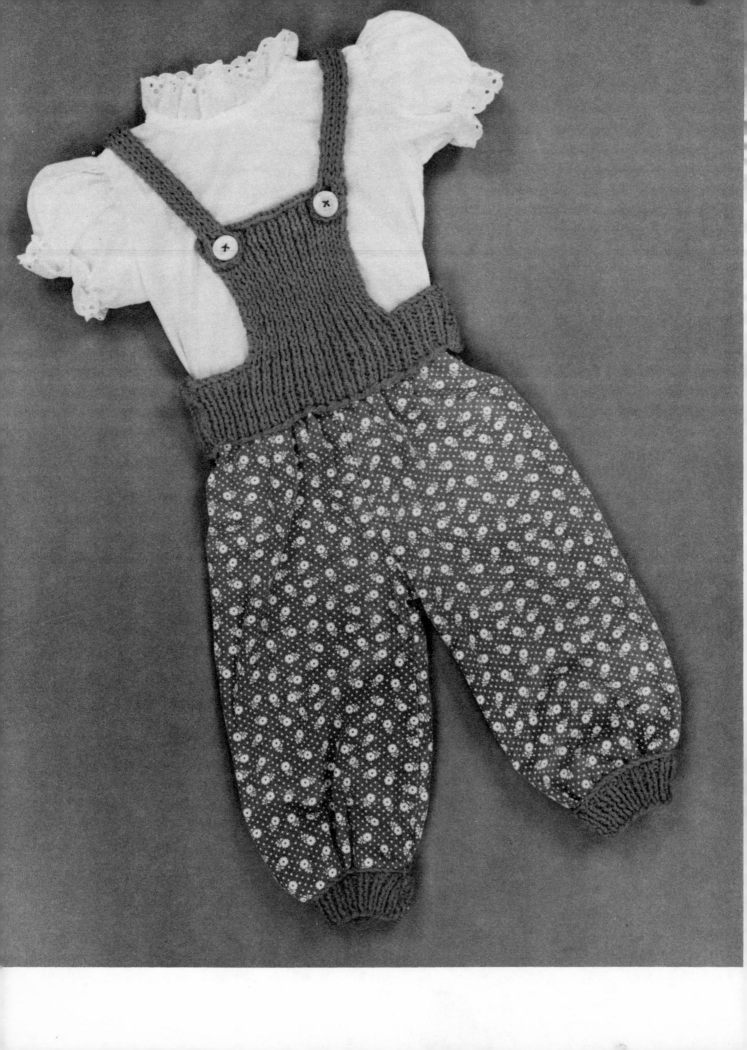

Leftover Overalls

Look at what one ball of acrylic sport yarn can do to your child's torn pants! With some simple knitting you can make a fresh-looking jumper with great ribbed cuffs. Those old pants will get some extra life; in fact, they'll look better than ever.

Size: For pants fitting 2 to 3 years.

Materials: Acrylic worsted-weight yarn, 3 oz red. Knitting needles No 6. Two buttons. One pair of used pull-on pants size 2, matching sewing thread.

Pattern stitch: Pat 1: rib 1/1: *K 1, P 1, rep from * across row.

Gauge: 15 sts = 4 inches = 23 rows (No 6 needles and Pat 1).

Note: Depending on size of pants, adjust the number of sts.

WAIST BORDER: With No 6 needles and red, cast on 94 sts. Work in Pat 1 for 2 inches.

FRONT BIB: Work as follows: Bind off first 39 sts, work across 16 center sts, and bind off last 39 sts. Continue on 16 center sts. Work even for 5 inches. Bind off sts.

SHOULDER STRAPS: With No 6 needles and red, cast on 5 sts. Work in Pat 1 until strap measures 15 inches in total length. *Next row:* Work a buttonhole of 1 st. *Next row:* Cast on 1 st over bound-off st. Work even in Pat 1 for 2 more rows. Bind off sts.

FINISHING: Sew leg border at lower edge of each leg, stretching the ribbing. Sew waist back seam. Cross straps in back. Sew each strap on inside waist 4 inches apart. Sew buttons on front bib.

Party Pants

Here's a delightful outfit made from your child's old pull-on pants. The sleeveless top has crocheted flowers, matching the pants used in this example. Of course, you can use this design simply as a model; let your creativity lead you to a unique pattern.

Size: For pants fitting 2 to 4 years.

Materials: 100 percent cotton worsted-weight yarn, 2.5 oz white (MC), 1 oz each pink and green. Knitting needles Nos 4 and 6. Crochet hook size F/5. A half yard of ½-inch-wide soft elastic for top. One pair of used pull-on pants.

Pattern stitch: Pat 1: rib 2/2: *K 2, P 2, rep from * across row. Pat 2: Seed st: *Row 1:* *K 1, P 1, rep from * across row. *Row 2:* *P 1, K 1, rep from * across row. Repeat rows 1 and 2.

Gauge: 24 sts = 4 inches = 34 rows (No 6 needles and Pat 2).

Finished measurements: Top: chest, 18 inches.

Note: Top is knitted in one piece.

TOP

With No 6 needles and MC, cast on 98 sts. Work in Pat 2 until piece measures 7½ inches in total length. Bind off sts loosely.

LEG BORDERS: With No 4 needles and MC, cast on 42 sts. In Pat 1 work for 1½ inches. Bind off sts in ribbing.

POCKET BORDER: With No 4 needles and MC, cast on 13 sts. In Pat 1 work for 1 inch. Bind off sts in ribbing.

FINISHING: Sew leg border at lower edge of each leg, stretching the ribbing. Sew pocket border edge, if there is one, or sew on upper part of pants as desired. Sew top side seam. With crochet hook and pink, work a row of sc around upper edge; join with a sl st. Change to green, work a second row of sc. Join with a sl st. Fasten off. Sew elastic inside upper edge, gathering to desired fit. Place top with seam on one side to inside waist of pants. Sew in place.

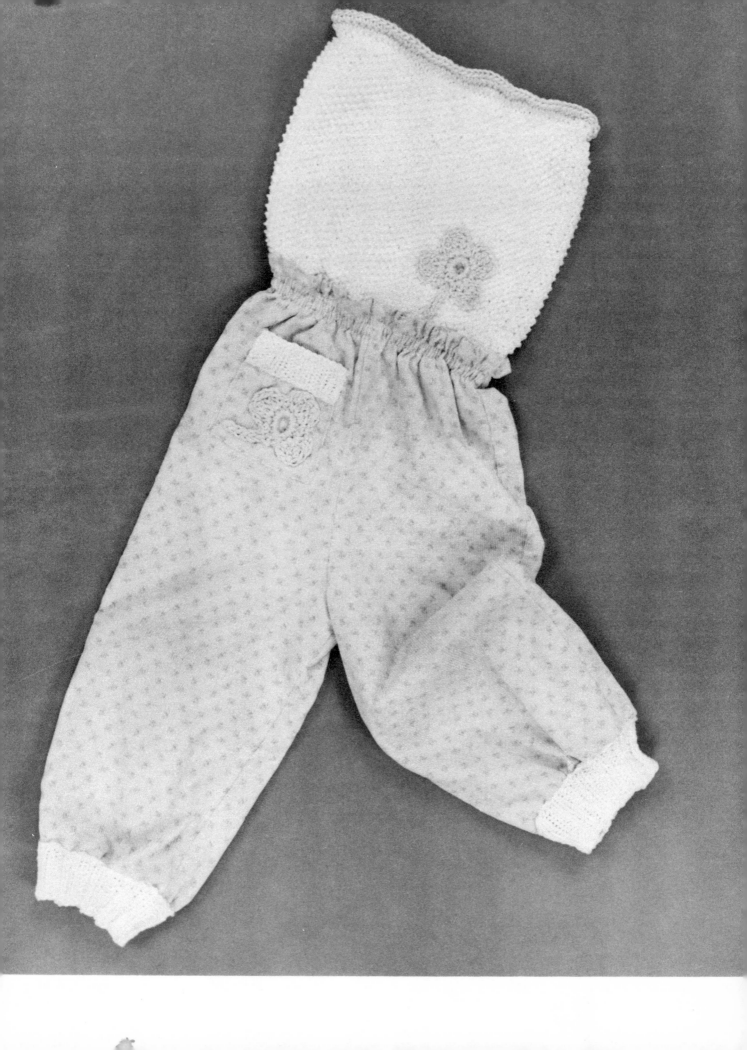

CROCHETED APPLIQUÉS

FLOWER I: With crochet hook and pink, ch 5, join with a sl st in a ring. *Rnd 1:* Ch 1, 13 sc in ring, join with a sl st to first ch. *Rnd 2:* Ch 1, 1 sc in next sc, *ch 4, **yo twice, insert hook in next st, yo, draw lp through (yo, draw through 2 lps) twice, rep from ** twice more in same st, yo, draw through 4 lps on hook, ch 3, 1 sc in each of next 2 sc, rep from * 3 times. **Stalk:** With hook and green, ch 7, turn; sl 1 st in each ch, 1 sl st in sc on flower.

FLOWER II: With hook and green, ch 8, join with a sl st in a ring. *Rnd 1:* Ch 1, 16 sc in ring, sl st to first ch. *Rnd 2:* Same work as for Flower I, working three petals only. **Stalk:** Same work as for first stalk.

FINISHING: Using sewing thread, sew on flowers and stalks as shown in photo.

Patches

What to do with leftover yarn? Knit or crochet some patches for all those pants and elbow holes you've been meaning to mend. They'll add color to the pants and sweaters and make efficient use of both yarn and your time. Any type of leftover wool, cotton, acrylic yarns will do just fine.

121

KNITTED KNEE AND ELBOW PATCHES

Materials: 100 percent wool worsted-weight yarn, 1 oz blue (MC), mohair worsted-weight yarn, .5 oz yellow (CC). Knitting needles No 4. Crochet hook size C/2. Matching sewing thread.

Pattern stitch: Pat 1: garter st: K every row.

ROUND SHAPE: With No 4 needles and MC, cast on 5 sts. Work in Pat 1 and inc 1 st at beg of next 2 rows, every other row, 9 times (= 23 sts). Work even for 20 rows. *Next row:* Dec 1 st at end of next 2 rows, every other row, 9 times. *Next row:* Bind off rem 5 sts. **Edging:**   With crochet hook and CC, work a row of sc around patch. Join with a sl st. Fasten off. Press lightly.

ELBOW PATCHES: With No 4 needles and MC, cast on 3 sts. Work in Pat 1 and inc 1 st at beg of next 2 rows, every other row, 6 times (= 15 sts). Work even for 10 rows. *Next row:* Dec 1 st at end of next 2 rows, every other row, 6 times. *Next row:* Bind off rem 3 sts. **Edging:**   With crochet hook and CC, work a row of sc around patch. Join with a sl st. Fasten off. Press lightly.

FINISHING: Using sewing thread, sew on knees and elbows.

CROCHETED KNEE PATCHES

Materials: Acrylic sport-weight yarn, 1 oz yellow (MC), 5 oz red (CC). Crochet hooks size D/3 and F/5. Matching sewing thread.

HEXAGON SHAPE: With crochet hook size F/5 and MC, ch 4. Join with a sl st in a ring. *Rnd 1:* Ch 1, 11 sc in next sc, 1 hdc in next sc, sl last st to first ch. *Rnd 2:* Ch 2, *3 hdc in next sc, 1 hdc in next sc, rep from * 4 times; 3 hdc in next sc, sl last st to second ch. *Rnd 3:* Ch 2, 1 hdc in next hdc, *3 hdc in next hdc, 1 hdc in each of next 3 hdc, rep from * 4 times, 3 hdc in next hdc, 1 hdc in next hdc, sl last st to second ch. *Rnd 4:* Ch 2, 1 hdc in each of next 2 hdc; *3 hdc in next hdc, 1 hdc in each of next 5 hdc, rep from * 4 times; 3 hdc in next hdc, 1 hdc in each of next 2 hdc; sl last st to second ch. Fasten off. **Edging:**   With crochet hook size D/3 and CC, work a row of sc around hexagon. Join with a sl st. Fasten off. Press lightly.

FINISHING: Using sewing thread, sew on knees.

How-To Section

HOW TO FOLLOW INSTRUCTIONS

Remember: Always read instructions in their entirety before starting a project.

Size: The finished measurements given in the instructions are for the largest size in the age range. However, as mentioned in the introduction, most of the clothes fit all children within the range beautifully.

Materials: Only general types of yarn are given for each pattern. You may buy any brand that you like, but be sure to work a swatch so that your brand matches that used in the instruction. Always buy a little extra yarn because dye lots change; the extras come in handy for alterations and mending.

Pattern Stitches: The various pattern stitches used to make a garment are abbreviated in the instructions as Pat 1, Pat 2 . . . Pat 3. For example, Pat 1 = stockinette stitch, Pat 2 = garter stitch. The stitches used with the accompanying abbreviation are clearly noted at the beginning of the instructions.

Gauge: Always work a swatch before starting a project to ensure that your gauge equals that given in the instructions. Make a swatch in the following way: Work a square of at least 4 inches by 4 inches in the given pattern stitch using the same size needles given in the instructions. Measure the square vertically (= rows) and horizontally (= stitches) by placing it flat and pinning it down. If there are more stitches and rows than in the instructions, use larger needles. If there are fewer, use smaller needles. Keep working until the exact gauge is obtained!

Reading and Working from Charts: Charts are used to simplify written instructions for jacquard patterns, multiple color patterns, geometrical shapes, or separate motifs. The chart is set on graph paper, and different symbols represent different colors. On the graph, one square equals one stitch, and one line of squares equals one row. To read a chart, start at the bottom right-hand corner. Reading from right to left gives the knit row (odd-numbered rows), and left to right gives the purl row (even-numbered rows).

Tips for Jacquards: A few simple reminders can make jacquard work easier. First, always change color on the "wrong" side of a work. Second, carry the color not being used loosely across the wrong side from edge to edge, twisting the strands of yarn every fifth stitch. Third, for separate large motifs, cut and join colors as needed. Finally, use bobbins for each color when working motifs and repetitive shapes.

TECHNIQUES

Horizontal Buttonholes: When you reach the place for the buttonhole, bind off the number of stitches required for the size of the button and work to the end of the row. At the next row, cast on the same number of stitches over the bound-off stitches and work to the end of the row. For wider buttonholes, sew a round in buttonhole stitch to reinforce the buttonhole.

Picking Up Stitches: Begin by working with the right side of the work facing you. Using knitting needles, pick up stitches onto the needle until you reach the end of the edge, making sure they are evenly spaced. With the second needle, work the pattern stitch as usual.

A crochet hook can also be used to pick up stitches by transferring each stitch to a knitting needle.

CROCHETED EDGES

Single Crochet Edges: This is the simplest way to finish a garment. On knitted piece, insert the hook from front to back in each stitch on bound-off or cast-on edges. Yarn over hook and draw through. Work a single crochet on each stitch.

Crocheted Picot Edges: I use picot edges in some of my garments to give a playful effect. To make them, simply do as follows: Work on right side of the work using a crochet hook. Make a single crochet stitch in each of the next three single crochet stitches, chain three stitches, and slip stitch into the last single crochet stitch made. Repeat this procedure to end of edge.

Curved Edges: Simply skip stitches in order to get a curved shape.

FRINGES

Cut strands of yarn to double the length of the desired tassel. Fold in half and, using a crochet hook, make a loop. Then pull the loop through the edge of the work to the right side. Tighten. Trim ends to desired length.

POMPONS

Cut two circles in cardboard of the diameter desired. Cut a smaller circle from the center of each piece. Put the two circles together and cover them, winding the yarn in and out. Place scissors between the edges of cardboard and cut all strands of yarn. Slip a strand of yarn between the two pieces, wind around tightly, and tie securely, leaving ends to attach the pompon. Pull away the cardboard, fluff up the pompon, and trim to desired shape.

EMBROIDERY STITCHES

Cross-Stitch: The stitch is worked in the same manner as on woven fabrics. Following a given chart, work a row of diagonal stitches starting on the left and moving to the right. Finish the crosses by working diagonal stitches in the opposite direction, right to left, across the row. Don't work the stitches too tightly or the garment will get out of shape.

Duplicate Stitch: This stitch imitates knitted work, and I use it as a decorative effect for small motifs, names, and numbers. It's worked on a stockinette stitch only, from the back side. Start at the bottom of the stitch to be embroidered and pull through to the front side. Next, slip the needle from right to left under the two loops of the stitch on the row above and pull through on front side. Then slip the needle back to the base of the stitch to be embroidered. Repeat the same procedure while following the motif to be embroidered.

Abbreviations

beg	begin(ning)
CC	contrasting color
ch(s)	chain(s)
dc	double crochet
dec	decrease(s) (ing)
dtr	double triple crochet
=	equals
gr	grams
hdc	half double crochet
in(s)	inch(es)
inc(s)	increase(s) (ing)
K	knit
lp(s)	loop(s)
MC	main color
No(s)	number(s)
oz	ounce(s)
P	purl
Pat(s)	pattern(s)
pc	picot
psso	pass slip stitch(s) over stitch(es)
rem	remaining
rep	repeat
rib	ribbing
rnd(s)	round
sc	single crochet
sl	slip
sl st	slip stitch
sp(s)	space(s)
st(s)	stitch(es)
St st	stockinette stitch
tog	together
tr	triple crochet
yo	yarn over
*(asterisk)	repeat directions following * as many times as directed
work even	work same pattern without increasing or decreasing

Measurements

CHEST-SIZE CHART

For Baby

AGE		CHEST	WEIGHT
B-1	newborn	to 18″	5 – 11 lbs.
B-2	6 months	to 20″	11 – 19 lbs.
B-3	1 year	to 22″	19 – 24 lbs.

For Child

AGE	CHEST
C-2	to 21″
C-3	to 22″
C-4	to 23″
C-5	to 24″
C-6	to 25″
C-7	to 26″
C-8	to 27″

DATE DUE

MAR 1 7 '84	NOV 27 '87			
MAR 3 0 '84	DEC - 3 1991			
APR 1 7 '84	1/11/94			
JUN 14 '84	FON			
MAR 12 '85				
Renew 3/26/85				
AUG 21 '85				
OCT 1 0 '86				
NOV 1 8 '86				
NOV 2 9 '95				

DEMCO 38-301

746.9 KAP

Kapstein, Claire Lacoste.

Fashion knitwear for
children /

3/84

CRAFTS

CANAJOHARIE LIBRARY & ART GALLERY

0 00 10 0010841 3

CANAJOHARIE LIBRARY
AND ART GALLERY